THE PLOTTERS

THE PLOTTERS

THE NEW YORK CONSPIRACY OF 1741

BY IRVING WERSTEIN

CHARLES SCRIBNER'S SONS / NEW YORK

This book
is for
Bert & Mim Obrentz

Cop. 2

"Hate is a fear and fear is rot
That cankers root and fruit alike . . ."

Robert Graves, *Hate Not, Fear Not*

AUTHOR'S NOTE

The tragic events of the 1741 "slave conspiracy" have obvious contemporary parallels. In our own time we have experienced mass hysteria, lynchings, murder, racial hatred, and "witch hunts" led by informers.

On the whole, this work is an accurate account of what happened more than two hundred years ago in New York City. The testimony of witnesses in court proceedings is taken from legal records.

I have consulted numerous sources to piece together the story of the so-called New York conspiracy. Most important of these were: the newspaper, *New York Weekly Journal* (1741), which provided interesting sidelights; the *History of the City of New York* (1867) was helpful, as were *The Letters and Papers of Cadwallader Colden* (9 vols.). *The Negro Plot of 1741* by Walter F. Prince, published in the *Saturday Chronicle*, New Haven, Conn. (1902) and *The New York Conspiracy, History of the Negro Plot,*

1741–1742 by Daniel Horsmanden, the presiding judge, gave complete accounts. The Horsmanden book, published in 1810, had invaluable details about the trials. *A History of Slavery in New York* by Edgar J. McManus (Syracuse University Press: 1966) contains a splendid condensed version of the events, as does Herbert Aptheker's *American Negro Slave Revolts* (Columbia University Press: 1943). Official documents and correspondence quoted in *The Plotters* are excerpted from the above mentioned source materials.

I wish to thank Dr. James J. Heslin, Director of the New York Historical Society, and his efficient library staff for the help I received while researching *The Plotters*. Mr. Gunther Pohl of the Local History and Genealogy Room, New York Public Library, went far beyond the demands of duty to assist me in my work. I owe him a special word of thanks.

Many people were ready with suggestions and advice. I now express my gratitude to them en masse. As always, my wife was patient when this crotchety author showed his worst side. My young son, Jack, forbore discussions with me about the merits of Willie Mays until working hours were over. For this, I now commend him.

I.W.

New York, June, 1966

PART ONE

BACKGROUND

"City without mercy . . ."

A plan of New York City in the English Period. 1750-1775. *Reproduced by the permission of the City History Club.* 18. The House of Correction. 19. City Prison. 26. Mount Pleasant. The sites of farms and country seats are shown by squares. Broken lines show present boundaries and landmarks of New York City.

ONE

New Yorkers who endured the winter of 1740–41 would never forget those bitter months or the tragic and dark time that followed the so-called "Hard Winter."

The weather remained fiercely cold from November, 1740, until April, 1741. Not even the oldest resident could recall anything that equaled the days of unrelenting arctic temperature.

On the outskirts of the city, cattle perished in pasture lands. Snow lay nearly six feet deep, clogging roads and isolating farms. Deer and wild game starved to death in the forests. It was said that birds plummeted from the sky, their wings glazed with ice.

On Manhattan Island, every stream, brook, and rivulet was frozen solid. Granite-hard ice coated the East River and the Hudson River. Huge floes choked the Bay, and people could drive to Staten Island in horse-drawn sleds across the icefields.

Death rode on wind and snow that winter in New York. Every day, victims of the cold were found dead on the streets, huddled in doorways, even within the shelter of their homes. A near-epidemic of pneumonia, bronchitis, and influenza raged and took its daily toll. Funeral corteges struggled through drifts to churchyard burying grounds, where work parties of thinly clad Negro slaves hacked out graves in the flinty ground. The task was so fatiguing that many of the diggers succumbed to exhaustion and died on the spot.

The rate of mortality ran especially high among poor whites and Negroes, for the "people in ruffles," as the affluent were called in the slang of the period, suffered mainly from inconveniences caused by the weather. The snow and cold were irksome, but the rich knew nothing of the hunger and disease besetting the lower classes.

The fine houses were snug, their storerooms well-stocked with hams, bacon, sausages, and smoked meats. Old wines filled racks in the cellars. Candle-lit chandeliers cast a gentle glow that was reflected by highly polished oaken floors. The opulence of the rich, their splendid clothes, elegant homes, their comfort and abundant food contrasted sharply with the poverty and squalor around them.

By the 1740's, New York City had a population of ten thousand, including some two thousand Negro slaves and an equal number of "white slaves"—indentured servants and workingmen. The bondsmen—black or white—lived in wretched hovels and shanties along the riverbanks or in dank alleyways. These miserable dwellings were not far

4

from the splendid houses of the city's merchants, bankers, and landlords. A world separated rich and poor—a social and economic gap that yawned like an abyss. Those on top cared nothing about the unfortunates living in the depths. The life or death of the ordinary people was of no consequence to ladies in silks and satins and gentlemen in powdered wigs and knee breeches.

In 1740, New York had been an English colony for more than seventy years. Known as New Amsterdam under Dutch rule, the city had expanded from a small settlement at Manhattan's southernmost tip into a bustling center of trade and commerce that matched Boston, Philadelphia, and Baltimore as a hub of the English colonies on the Atlantic seaboard.

New York's waterfront was crowded with ships flying the flags of many nations. Docks were piled high with crates, boxes, and barrels. Porters trundled handcarts up and down gangplanks. Along the East River piers, all was noise, confusion, and busy scurrying. Vans, lorries, and drays rolled through narrow streets to and from the piers; people jostled each other on walks where peddlers called out a variety of wares.

Amid all this busy commercial activity, herdsmen drove cattle up Broadway, to graze less than a mile north of the city hall. Pigs rooted and goats nibbled grass in City Hall Park, which was known as "The Fields." Just west of Broadway, in the vicinity of St. Paul's Church, King's Farm and Annetje Jans' Farm, where slaves tilled fields and tended flocks, sprawled to the banks of the Hudson River.

Since the era of the Dutch, the city had pushed north more than a mile to Grand Street, which ran from the Hudson River shore to the East River marshes. Cobblestone-paved Broadway started at the Battery, ran in a northerly direction for a short distance, and became a winding dirt wagon road that terminated at Bloomingdale Village, some six miles away.

About halfway down Grand Street rose Mount Pleasant, from the top of which one could overlook the city. Below lay a large fresh-water lake called "The Collect," because so many springs and streams fed it. The lake covered a wide expanse in the vicinity of Chatham Square. A large island in the middle of The Collect was the site of legal hangings and other executions.

Manhattan Island, as seen from the top of Mount Pleasant, had swamps, woodlands, and fields. Trout and other fish abounded in Minetta Water, a tumbling brook that cut through the region known as Greenwich, where many rich New Yorkers had country estates.

On surveyors' maps, cross streets were shown laid out up to 59th Street—however, they existed only on paper. Above Grand Street, rambling paths and trails traversed the Island through thick forests that were full of deer and game. Trappers snared beaver in swamp and stream and sold the valuable pelts to dealers in the commercial district only a few miles south.

Almost all Manhattan was covered by the wilderness that fringed the city. The Island's southern end, where Fort George with its garrison, the Governor's House, the

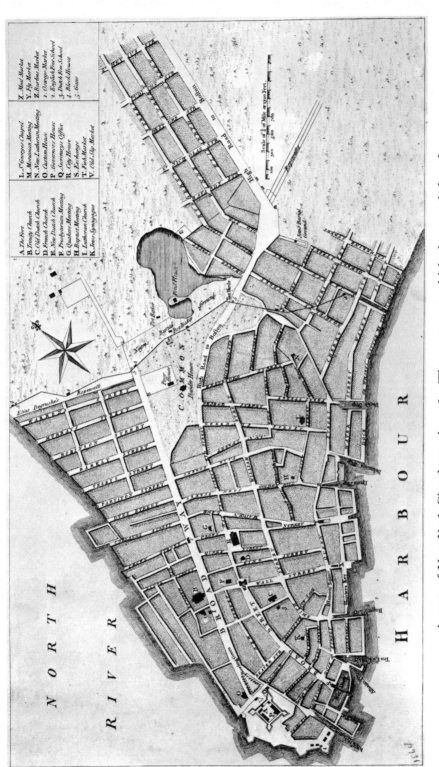

A map of New York City drawn in 1763. The survey on which the map is based was made some years earlier, and New York changed very little in the 1740's and 1750's. *I. N. Phelps Stokes Collection of American Historical Prints.*

Customs House, and other buildings formed a military and administrative enclave, was the most heavily populated region.

Adjoining this section were clustered neat, gabled one-story brick houses of Dutch design. Only a short walk away stood low drinking dives, grogshops, and taverns where sailors, dockworkers, slaves, and white bondsmen came to drink whisky, at a penny a glass, or cheap rum. These dens were trouble spots. Knives flashed in nightly brawls. Killings were commonplace. Soldiers, wielding bayonets and muskets, often had to break up the murderous disorders.

Outside the drinking spots, ragged five- and six-year-old beggar children prowled in muddy alleys and narrow lanes. Older boys and girls picked pockets, snatched purses, and stole anything they could carry easily. Gangs of bandit urchins preyed on passersby, beating and robbing them, even though the loot was rarely more than a few pennies in poverty-stricken neighborhoods. There were no Robin Hoods in those robber bands; the poor took from the poor in an urban jungle.

Not even the most prominent person was safe from the undercurrents of danger and violence. Only the boldest of men ventured out after dark, when footpads and muggers menaced the city. If a man had to leave home at night, he went armed with pistol, cudgel, or sword.

Housebreakings, holdups, and robberies took place almost daily. The night watch that patrolled the streets could not cope with the flood of crime. Not even the severe penalties imposed for stealing served as a deterrent. Although a person could be flogged, mutilated, or branded "at the discretion of the court" for committing even minor crimes, the rate kept soaring. A felony, such as burglary, brought a mandatory death sentence, carried out by hanging, burning at the stake, or breaking on the wheel. In colonial New York, justice was more like vengeance than legal punishment.

Too often, poor whites and Negroes suffered punishments that far outweighed their crimes. Men were sometimes hanged for stealing a loaf of bread. Boys and girls in their teens were frequently publicly flogged for petty mischief. Justice miscarried with appalling frequency. Once a twenty-year-old Negro servant girl, accused of stealing some jewelry from her mistress, was arrested, tried, convicted, and hanged on The Collect Island within forty-eight hours. Her body was left to dangle at the end of a rope and decompose in the sun.

The day after her execution, the missing baubles were found. Her mistress had misplaced them. When the judge who had passed sentence learned of this, he merely shrugged. He refused to order that the corpse be cut down and given a decent burial.

"Let her hang there as a warning to every Black in New York," he said. "That putrefying cadaver will serve as an example to any mischief-minded Black that a dire fate awaits wrongdoers in this city!"

Few whites were perturbed that the girl had not received a fair trial, that her death was legalized murder. No voice was raised against the judge who had doomed her.

9

No one brought to task the prosecutor for pressing a case without evidence, witnesses, or a chance for the defendant to prove her innocence. It mattered only that the accused had a black skin and her accuser was white.

Negroes, according to a leading New Yorker, " . . . must be shown no mercy . . . else our slaves, mistaking leniency for weakness, will rise and destroy us. . . . " Such words revealed the obsessive fear that poisoned the minds of slaveowners in New York. They were terrified of their slaves.

This dread had been gnawing at slaveowners throughout the English colonies for decades. They feared that the Negroes and their white counterparts, oppressed indentured bondsmen, would one day revolt.

In the past, there had been several sporadic outbursts, each crushed by ruthless force. Negroes had been beaten to death, burned at the stake, shot, broken on the wheel, and hanged. The panic-stricken whites had not cared that innocent and guilty alike were slaughtered. In fact, only a handful of slaves ever had joined the insurrections. The extent of the uprisings was exaggerated by hysterical slaveowners. To them, every Negro was a potential menace; before reason and logic were restored, innocent Negroes were legally massacred.

The most recent slave "uprising" in New York had taken place in April, 1712. Troops were sent to put down the disorders that erupted in a slave quarter. The soldiers subdued the Negroes without any difficulty, but the cry went up that "the Blacks were rising."

10

Governor Robert Hunter, pressed by a group of prominent citizens, began investigation of the minor disturbances. It should have been dismissed for what it was— a minor riot—but the idea of a full-scale Negro revolt so haunted the Governor's committee that it reported that a slave plot "to slay all white men, women, and children in this city . . . " had been uncovered.

Scores of Negroes were arrested and subjected to torture. Soon many admitted their complicity in the plot, and twenty-one slaves were pointed out as ringleaders of the conspiracy. The grand jury returned indictments, and the court swiftly condemned all the defendants to death.

A large crowd ringed the shores of The Collect, and small boats dotted the water on the day of the hangings. Cheers sounded when the bodies swung from the gallows in the mild April breezes. Evidence against the condemned had been based on hearsay, but New Yorkers demanded scapegoats, and the slaves filled the role. As one prominent citizen remarked: "The Blacks must from time to time be reminded that we are the masters. . . . I can think of nothing more effective than measures such as this to drive home the lesson. . . . I am certain we shall have little trouble from the Blacks for some time to come. . . . "

The Negroes executed in 1712 joined the ranks of the hapless men, women, and children murdered by fear-goaded whites. The slaveowners had been apprehensive of their charges ever since 1628, in the New Amsterdam days, when Dutch burghers had imported Africans to "toil in the fields and to till the land. . . . "

11

The importation of slaves under the Dutch was not very great. The slave trade increased after the English took over. By the opening of the eighteenth century, it was a substantial business. Trafficking in Negroes proved highly lucrative. The captains of slave ships made huge fortunes; slave traders and dealers grew wealthy buying and selling Africans. Since slavery was practiced on a racial basis, all black-skinned people were branded as fit only to be chattels. A good price were put upon them—a healthy Negro brought two hundred dollars or more on the auction block.

In 1709, a slave mart was built at the foot of Wall Street, and there, twice weekly, more frequently if the supply was great, Negroes were sold to the highest bidder. Despite the total power of life and death the whites held over the slaves, they never quite lost their dread of the Negroes. One historian has pointed out that this feeling undoubtedly stemmed from a "deep sense of guilt" the whites had; as Christians they knew slavery to be wrong, perhaps even sinful; owning slaves put them in the category of barbarians, not civilized men.

But slavery was considered an economical means of supplying labor, and in years to come many Negroes acquired skills—they became bootmakers, blacksmiths, mechanics, and carpenters, thus earning the enmity and hatred of white indentured workers who saw them as a threat to their own status.

White bondsmen and black slaves were pitted against each other in fierce competition for jobs; once a white man had completed his period of indenture, he was ostensibly "free" to work for wages. The employers soon realized that by using slaves they forced free whites to work for lower pay.

But this merciless economic rivalry was still far in the future. During the first half of the eighteenth century, some white workers had gained "freedom" from the indentured service to which they had committed themselves. In New York, Negroes and poor whites often made common cause. But having a white skin gave a man certain advantages over the Negro—trial by jury, a chance to vote, and, above all, the knowledge that someday he would be at liberty to come and go as he pleased. This no slave could even hope to attain unless his master set him free—which was a most unlikely event.

Although there were many laws on the books governing the control of slaves, even harsher restrictions, known as the "Black Codes," were enacted after the bloody incidents of April, 1712.

Under the Black Codes, more than three Negroes could not assemble in one place "except for purposes of Christian worship . . . and then only [with] proper super-, vision. . . . " An infraction of this rule made an offender liable to forty lashes "on the bared back."

Death was summarily prescribed for any "Negro slave or freeman found in possession of a weapon . . . including but not limited to a cudgel, knife, saber, sword, dagger, pistol, fowling piece, musket or pike. . . . "

Under the Black Codes, the death penalty also was

mandatory should "any black male or female for any reason whatsoever commit assault upon any white person of either sex whether bondsman, indentured servant, freeman, Christian or Jew. . . . "

For the purposes of the law, assault was defined as "threatening a white man, woman or child by look, gesture, speech or implication. . . . " A slave convicted of assault was to be executed by "hanging, flogging or burning at the stake, according to the pleasure of the Court. . . . "

The Black Codes were sternly enforced, and slaves were flogged or executed under one or another of the Code's provisions. The oppressive legislation apparently proved effective; after 1712 there was no further alarm about a Negro "insurrection," although the possibility of one still hounded New Yorkers.

During the first week of 1740, an unusual incident took place in the city's main market, The Fly Mart, located on Queen Street. One morning a strange person appeared there—a gaunt, bearded man who wore flowing robes and carried a shepherd's crook. His bony feet were shod in sandals. Striding through the crowd of shoppers, he cried thunderously, "Thou art lost! Thou art doomed! I see blood and fire! Ashes and ruin!"

Customers and tradespeople listened aghast to this dire prediction. The stranger glared about him with eyes that "burned like hot coals," according to an onlooker. "He seemed, for all the world, like an angry prophet out of the Old Testament," another observer wrote. "Who he was or whence he came, we knew not . . . but his voice and

14

presence sent a chill of fear through all who heard and saw him. . . . "

Before anyone dared move, the bearded man stalked away, turned a corner, and disappeared.

Within an hour, the news crackled from one end of the city to the other. All sorts of fanciful touches were added, until the truth became completely distorted. Some swore the stranger had "disappeared in a sheath of flame as had the Prophet Elijah." Many believed he was a divine messenger sent to warn the city's populace of future disaster. A few labeled him a Spanish agent spying out the city's defenses—a naval war had broken out between England and Spain, and everyone was jittery about an attack by the Spanish fleet. There were those who ridiculed the whole affair, claiming that the man was a religious fanatic. However, no one could guess where he had gone, nor was he ever seen again. The skeptics pointed out that the beard and the clothes might have been a disguise quite easily discarded. In any case, for days after the Fly Mart incident worshipers crowded the churches and the city's only synagogue, as New Yorkers were caught up in an unprecedented wave of piety.

Despite the outpourings of prayer, a series of peculiar circumstances befell New York City. About mid-January, the weather turned so balmy that trees started budding and spring flowers poked out of the thawed ground months ahead of time. Days and weeks of an almost tropical climate paraded in unbroken sequence.

At first New Yorkers saw nothing ominous in the unusual weather. They enjoyed the sunshine at that gray season, but as the hot spell continued unabated through January, February, March, April, and beyond, people began to grow uneasy. No rain fell from mid-January until mid-August. Nothing like this had ever happened before, and everyone remembered the stranger's prophecy.

The drought was proving a catastrophe. Fields once green and lush in springtime were burned as though put to the torch. The rye, wheat, barley and corn that should have been ripening stood sere and withered in the arid earth. Rich soil turned to dry dust. Farmers gazed anxiously at the sky but could see no promise of rain.

As if the drought were not bad enough, there was a further affliction. Ships lay idle in port awaiting favorable winds that never blew. Sails hung limply in the hot, humid air. Cargoes moldered in holds. Without wind to propel them, incoming merchantmen drifted in the doldrums.

Slave ships carrying Negroes from Africa to New York suffered severely. Packed below decks without air or fresh water, the slaves perished of suffocation or thirst as potable water ran out. The crew of one slave ship towed the vessel for days through the glass-smooth sea by lowering the longboats and rowing. But one by one the oarsmen collapsed. The skipper died at the helm. Somehow the imprisoned Negroes managed to break open a hatch. They tumbled out on deck, only to meet death from hunger and thirst.

Weeks later the death ship ran aground on the New England coast. The men of a fishing village boarded her.

Shocked by the sight of the corpses, they set the ill-fated ship afire; she burned and smoldered for days like a floating funeral pyre.

The slave traders of New York mourned their lost profits when they finally learned the ship's fate. The Negroes would have brought high prices on the auction block.

All businessmen in New York suffered sharp financial setbacks. With shipping brought to a standstill, there were neither imports nor exports. Perishables awaiting transport rotted on docks or in warehouses. Many firms were on the verge of bankruptcy; an aura of gloom and despair blanketed the city. In addition to bringing economic woes, the drought was swiftly creating a health hazard. A water shortage loomed, as streams and brooks dried up.

Soon the level of The Collect, which supplied much of the city's fresh water, fell to an alarmingly low mark. Many fish were stranded in the mud by the receding waters. As the fish died, a stench rose from the lake, a noxious odor that hung over the city, tainting and befouling the air. Doctors glumly predicted an outbreak of spotted fever or some other plague.

A wild tale began circulating: The Collect had been poisoned with a deadly concoction prepared by an ancient colored woman, a wrinkled crone named Hagar, who was reputed to be a witch. Years before, she had been a slave but her master had set Hagar free as he lay dying. The old woman lived alone in a shanty on the western edges of the

17

wide Salt Marshes near Corlear's Hook. No one knew her age; some claimed she was more than a hundred years old. Among the slaves, it was widely believed that she had supernatural powers and in her native Haiti had been a voodoo priestess.

Slaves came to her miserable hut for philters, potions, charms, and powders to cure illnesses or injure enemies. There were awed rumors that Hagar held unholy rites deep inside the Salt Marshes where few ever had ventured. At these forbidden ceremonies Hagar allegedly performed acts of voodoo magic that no eyewitness dared describe on pain of becoming a "zombie"—a living dead man. No one actually knew what went on at these conclaves in the Marshes or whether anything really took place. But despite the absence of concrete evidence, Hagar was generally believed to be a necromancer, witch, and sorceress.

When the foul smell rose from The Collect, men said Hagar had put a curse on the lake; others thought she had poisoned the water. The heat and the drought were her black magic. Who knew what blackness and evil the old witch on the Marshes was preparing?

In July a young woman collapsed after drinking water out of a bucket that had been filled at The Collect. No link existed between the water and the girl who had fainted, but the seeds of panic had been planted. Although she promptly recovered and went on her way, an outcry arose that she had died of poisoning. Staid business men, citizens who were usually level and clear-headed, reacted without reason or logic. This was the threat the stranger in the Fly

A view of the Collect. *I. N. Phelps Stokes Collection of American Historical Prints.*

Mart had predicted. Poisoning The Collect was only the first move in a desperate conspiracy by the slaves to take over New York. The fear of another "uprising," like the one in 1712, rose to ridiculous heights. Old New Yorkers told elaborate lies about the extent of that abortive "plot."

Rich townsmen packed up their families and fled to Greenwich, Bloomingdale, Brooklyn, Jersey, or Long Island. Long columns of carts and carriages lurched along bumpy roads, the horses kicking up dust clouds that soon powdered drivers and passengers. Everything, everyone choked on dryness.

Those remaining in the city avoided drinking water from The Collect. They bought water sold by vendors who drove about the streets calling: "Water, water, sweet and pure! Spring water, fresh and clear! Sixpence the quart! Water! Sweet water!"

They did not lack customers, who came with pots and jars to buy the water ladled out of the peddler's casks. It was claimed that the water had been hauled down from isolated springs at the northern end of the island. "I have a source known only to a few," a seller might tell a customer. "An old Indian guided me to this spring." (Actually, the casks were filled at The Collect each night.)

Days rolled by in discomfort and tension. Whites eyed Negroes suspiciously, seeking the slightest hint of an insurrection. The slaves worked and fretted about the future. They knew that the water shortage, crop failure, and the chance of an epidemic boded a dark time for them. Negroes and indentured whites would suffer most from hunger, thirst, and disease. The poor, not the "people in ruffles," were destined to be the main victims.

The blistering summer dragged on without respite. In August, New York was an inferno; the sun beat down pitilessly and the nights brought no relief. The water level of The Collect fell lower and lower. In the woods so many streams went dry that deer and forest animals emerged to search for water. They found The Collect, and according to a letter written by a New York printer:

"There came a nightly parade of wild creatures to slake their thirsts. . . . They cast aside all natural timidity and boldly approached the water. . . . It was a sight, I believe, unequalled since the time of Noah, for animals of all sorts, natural foes, stood side by side, enmities forgotten, instincts overcome in their mutual distress. . . ."

The drought ended as abruptly as it had struck, with an eerie touch of the supernatural. One night, during the second week in August, somebody crept into Hagar's shanty, murdered the old woman while she slept, and set the place afire. Flames danced in the darkness of the Marshes; for a few moments the hut burned like a pine-tar torch. The blaze caused great fear in the city. Surely, this must be the prophecy of the stranger in the Fly Mart coming true.

Blood and fire. Ashes and ruin. The terrible words seemed to echo in the night. All at once, the walls of the hut collapsed and the roof crashed to the ground. A column of sparks showered up like swarming red fireflies. Onlookers drew cautiously closer, for by now everyone was aware that the burning shack had been Hagar's. They approached warily, poised to bolt, fearful that this might be some more of her black magic.

When nothing unusual happened, a few men, bolder than the rest, began to poke about in the ruins by the light of the flickering flames. The searchers found Hagar's charred remains, and as they clustered around, a lightning streak ripped the sky, followed by a loud thunderclap.

The crowd shouted in terror and fled blindly. "It's her! It's Hagar's doing!" a man screamed. Some ran into the marsh, floundering through canebrake and mud. Others, galvanized by fear, stampeded into the city. They were convinced that the lightning and thunder had been more of the "witch's deviltry" and were harbingers of doomsday.

That night, an electrical storm buffeted New York. Great shafts of lightning flashed to a background of thunder. Townspeople cowered as eye-searing flashes lit the heavens and thunderbolts shook the earth. At times, lightning struck trees, which disappeared in sheaths of white-hot fire. Flames spread, and a dozen blazes danced through the woods, casting a red glow against the heavily clouded sky. The small fires merged to form a huge conflagration that roared through the dry forest and swept on toward the city itself.

The Fly Mart prophet had spoken the truth. There had been blood and fire; now would follow ashes and ruin.

TWO

No barrier stood between the city and the fire, which advanced like a burning tidal wave. New York seemed on the verge of doom. Then a tremendous flash of lightning rent the night and the thunder that reverberated in its wake seemed to "split the earth," according to one observer:

"It was as though both earth and sky had been splintered . . . . I was at a window of my house staring in horror at the onrushing fire racing full tilt in my direction when the lightning glare momentarily blinded me . . . . I fell to my knees as the thunder shook the walls, for I believed this was Judgement Day . . . ."

Many others prayed that night when everything seemed hopeless. Perhaps their supplications were answered; moments after the lightning and thunder, rain cascaded upon the parched city. It was a torrential downpour that fell in drenching sheets. The deluge drowned the fire in the forest and saved New York from catastrophe. That storm ended the drought and marked a new weather cycle. A heavy rain fell almost daily. Dried up stream beds gurgled again; brooks that had been reduced to a trickle became raging cataracts. The Collect overflowed its banks and The Marshes, where Hagar had lived, became a vast, soggy swampland.

The days of late August, September, and October were sunless. Gray clouds formed a somber overhead curtain. The damp and chilly air added to an almost universal feeling of gloom and despondency.

23

"Damn this eternal rain!" a New Yorker, exploded in a letter to a Virginia friend. "I do truly believe we shall grow webbed feet, for only an amphibian can survive this infernal clime!"

The mud was nearly knee-deep in the streets. Vehicles sank to the hubcaps. Horses were mired. Pedestrians slithered and sloshed through the claylike muck. The rains seldom slackened, and deep puddles filled roadways. Rain water seeped into houses, weakened foundations, and flooded cellars. Strong winds constantly lashed the harbor and rivers, and anchored ships rocked perilously at their moorings. The gales stirred up gigantic waves that pounded The Battery seawall, and breakers crashed over it, sending gallons of water into bunkers and magazines. Cursing soldiers had to move shot and powder to higher ground, and no sooner had mop and bucket brigades cleaned up than other waves caused fresh floods.

The abominable weather was the city's main topic of conversation. Slaves huddled at night in their mean quarters muttering ancient tribal incantations to exorcise Hagar's evil spirits that were causing the rain. As the foul days continued, the Negroes fell back on dimly recalled rites of the old jungle gods. Weirdly painted dancers whirled and leaped to the throbbing cadence of drums.

The drums irked and frightened the whites. "Such pagan rituals only serve to enflame our slaves," a merchant wrote. "It is claimed that their only purpose is to drive out the "spirits" that are responsible for this period of inclement weather . . . . As a Christian I frown upon such heathen practises . . . . I am fearful the Blacks may become so aroused that they will murder us in the night . . . . I and other of the gentry have petitioned Sir George Clarke, the Governor, to prohibit such unsavory doings in the immediate future . . . . His Excellency has assured us that proper measures will be taken to end them . . . ."

Clarke's measures characterized his treatment of Negroes. Soldiers haphazardly rounded up some slaves who were brought to court, found guilty of violating the Black Codes, and sentenced to public flogging. Among the unlucky Negroes were some young boys and girls, whose youth did not save them from the punishment.

A large audience gathered in the rain to watch the floggings, which were administered on the Fort George parade ground. Each prisoner was to receive forty lashes. Two—a seventeen-year-old girl and a boy of twelve—died from the lashing.

After this, no more drums were heard in the night. Outwardly there was no evidence of the slaves' anger, but it seethed beneath the seemingly placid surface. Men more sensitive or astute than New York's officials would have recognized the temper of the slaves, but the complacent authorities did not bother to delve. As long as the slaves worked hard and "kept in line," all was well.

Judge John Chambers, who had sentenced the Negroes to be flogged, stated, "Our Blacks will not turn again to false gods . . . the whip has exorcised the pagan demons and I believe the black seed of Cain among us now will walk in the footsteps of Our Lord. . . . "

The rainy period ceased abruptly. On the last day of October, 1740, the temperature plunged well below freezing, and winter came in with howling winds and a snowstorm. The crippling cold would last until the following April, and a time of dreadful suffering started for the city's poor.

Negroes seeking warmth went to tippling dives and grogshops on Vesey Street and Water Street in defiance of the Black Codes. Here at least they found a fire and some companionship. A man needed only a penny or two for a noggin of rum to warm his bones.

The drinkers ran little risk of being arrested. Soldiers stayed in their barracks, and the night patrol seldom made its rounds in the extreme cold. The slaves and the white bondsmen guzzled rum and cursed the rich; driven by want and misery, they grew desperate.

PART TWO

THE DARK TIME

"The mills of God grind slowly . . ."

ONE

At a few minutes before midnight on Friday, February 28,
1741, Mr. Robert Hogg, a well-to-do tobacconist, was
awakened by a noise in his home on Broad Street. He listened for a few moments, not sure what had aroused him
from sleep. As usual, the wind was buffeting the house and
cold permeated the room; the bedchamber fire had long
since burned out.

Hogg thought that the disturbing sounds might have
been the wind rattling the shutters or whistling through
the eaves. He was reluctant to leave his warm bed; his wife,
sleeping beside him under the feather comforter, had not
stirred.

The tobacconist was about to drop off again when he
heard a muffled cough in the parlor below. Sitting up
quickly, he slid open a drawer of the bedside night table.
His fingers curled around the butt of the loaded pistol he always kept there. Gripping the weapon, Hogg

slipped out of bed without awakening his wife. He padded barefoot across the floor to the staircase and peered down through the darkness.

Moonlight shimmered off the snow banked outside and cast a dim light into the parlor through the lead glass windows. Hogg saw a shadowy movement and shouted, "You there! Stand fast or I'll shoot!"

Shoes scrambled across the oaken floor, and in the faint glow Hogg glimpsed a man dashing for the door with a sack slung over his shoulder. He shot at the fleeing intruder. The explosion was deafening, and a cloud of powder smoke swirled up. Behind him, Hogg's wife screamed. The man yanked the front door open, and an icy blast filled the house.

Hogg ran to the entrance, ignoring the cold and the powdery snow that blew in from the door, but the thief was swallowed up by the night. Thinly clad and without shoes, Hogg could not chase him. He turned back to the parlor and slammed the door. From the head of the stairs, his wife cried, "Robert! Robert! What happened?"

"It was a thief," he replied.

"A thief!" she shrieked and crumpled to the floor in a dead faint.

Hogg lit a candle with fumbling fingers and dashed up to his prostrate wife. He was kneeling beside her when someone pounded on the door and an excited voice yelled, "Hogg! Open up! What's going on?"

He hurried down and admitted his neighbor, Silas Lupton, a tallowmaker. Lupton waved a pistol and gasped, "I heard a shot. Came fast as I could throw some clothes on. What's wrong?"

"A housebreaker. I came on him red-handed, but then he got away."

More people rushed in with coats thrown over night clothes. Several of the men carried weapons. They milled about, tracking snow across the parlor rug, talked loudly about forming a safety committee, denounced the governor, the city officials, and the weather, but made no move to go after the robber. The women took care of Julia Hogg, who promptly went off into a fit of hysterics after she was revived. Her loud wailing finally subsided when the doctor arrived and gave her a sleeping draught.

A practical man, Hogg ignored all the fuss and drew up an inventory of his losses. They were substantial. The thief had taken a good haul. The loot included money, an expensive silver service, and some costly table linens.

Someone went to the Fort and brought back a squad of sleepy soldiers led by a disgruntled sergeant. The noncom asked a few questions, complained about being disturbed for such a trivial matter, and marched his men back to the barracks. A city constable appeared, poked around, and then departed. Such robberies were common in New York, and at the time nobody suspected that the Hogg case would be the first in a series of events that were to have a shocking aftermath for the city.

The next night, Saturday, March 1, another house was entered. This time the thief broke into a jewelry shop owned by Abraham Myers Cohen, who lived with his pretty wife, Esther, in a comfortable apartment above the store. Cohen's place was located off Pearl Street near the Golden Hill district, in a narrow block called Jews' Alley, because most of the city's Jews lived and did business there.

The robber jimmied open the shop's rear door and was putting rings, watches, and silver candlesticks into a gunny sack, when Esther Cohen, carrying a lighted lantern, came downstairs. She had just time enough to scream before the intruder stunned her with a punch on the jaw. As Abraham came charging down, brandishing an iron poker, the intruder dropped his sack and fled. Shouting for help, Cohen chased the thief but lost him.

The uproar awakened all Jew's Alley. The residents gathered in Cohen's shop. As on the previous night, nothing seemed extraordinary about the burglary except that it had been bungled. But when Esther regained her senses, she added an alarming sidelight to the incident. The thief, she swore, had been a Negro. "I saw him in the lantern's ray before he hit me," she insisted. The word skipped from one person to another. A Black had done it! This was indeed a serious affair.

Despite New York's high crime rate, only a few crimes were committed by Negroes; not many slaves dared defy the Black Codes—not when robbery was a capital offense. The man who had broken into Cohen's store would surely pay with his life for slugging Esther; he had violated the Codes twice—once for robbery, the second time for hitting a white person.

With the robber identified as a Negro, even the indolent officials were spurred into action. Patrols from Fort George and city constables hunted vainly for the culprit. Although the Cohens were Jews and the object of some prejudice, no white man could be indifferent about the attack on Esther. If a Negro struck a white woman and went unpunished, then no one was safe, they reasoned. The guilty slave had to be caught, for while he was at large, every white woman in New York feared for her safety.

The intensive search turned up nothing; not a single clue to the identity of the housebreaker was uncovered. The authorities were stumped. In desperation, a member of the city council proposed that any two Negroes be arrested and executed for the crimes, but this proposal was turned down. The reason was not based on humanitarian or legal grounds but plain economics. Since each member of the council owned slaves, he balked at the idea of endangering another slaveholder's financial investment by offhandedly destroying his property. "Were we even faintly certain of a Black's guilt, not one of us would shrink from sending him to his death. But none among us cares to squander another man's money," a council member wrote.

The hunt went on; soldiers and constables poked, prodded, and probed without success. Then, about a week after the robbery, Hogg remembered that a white sailor named Christopher Wilson had happened to enter his shop while Julia was counting gold coins—the day's receipts. Wilson had demanded some tobacco but had no money. He was drunk and Hogg had been forced to throw him out of the place. The sailor had flown into a fury. Hogg remembered him shouting, "All you rich are alike! Everything for yourselves and nothing for the poor! Well, damn it, I'll make you sweat! You'll regret treating Chris Wilson like a dog!"

The sailor, who had been arrested in the past for drunken brawling, was known to be friendly with Negroes. Although this was not much to go on, Attorney General Richard Bradley had a warrant issued for Wilson's arrest.

A dragnet was spread for the sailor. The constables and soldiers sought him in "tippling dives," taverns, and grogshops. The man was finally found in a low den on Little Dock Street and hauled off to the city prison near City Hall Park. Befuddled by drink, the sailor was confronted and accused of robbing Hogg.

The charge so startled Wilson that he sobered up almost at once. Denying any knowledge of the crime, he vowed that his threat to Hogg had been pure bluster. However, he admitted telling two slaves, Prince and Caesar, about the gold coins he had seen Mrs. Hogg counting.

According to Wilson, the day after the robbery he had come across them in the White Rose, a tavern on Vesey Street, one of the city's most notorious dives and a rendezvous for some of the city's roughest elements. Soldiers, sailors, thugs, bondsmen, pickpockets, slaves, and assorted criminals used the place as a hangout. Prince and Caesar, Wilson claimed, had "a hatful of gold coins" and bought him a bottle of rum for tipping them off about Hogg's money.

Attorney General Bradley knew the White Rose well. The owner, John Hughson, had been fined many times for serving Negroes in his establishment. Despite these penalties, Hughson refused to bar Negroes from the premises. His reasons were purely selfish ones. He ran a side business—John Hughson was a "fence"—a receiver of stolen goods. Since slaves often pilfered from their masters, he wanted them as customers. A Negro could get a few shillings from Hughson for the loot—money he promptly put back into the tavern keeper's pocket by spending it on drinks.

Acting as a receiver for stolen goods was punishable by death in colonial New York, and Attorney General Bradley often had tried to pin Hughson as a fence. But no incriminating evidence ever was found. For the record, Hughson's only lawbreaking was allowing the sale of liquor to Negroes in his tavern—a minor charge at worst and one widely practiced in the city. The ordinance was loosely enforced, and most of the low-class tippling dives served slaves.

Acting on the strength of Wilson's statement, Bradley arrested Prince, Caesar, and John Hughson. The tavern owner was charged with being the fence for the stolen silverware and linens. Bradley arbitrarily accused Prince of the Hogg robbery while Caesar was blamed for entering Cohen's house and striking Esther.

Because he had no solid evidence against the slaves, Bradley put them in solitary confinement in the basement of the city prison, a damp, dank hole. Despite beatings, mistreatment, and a bread-and-water diet, both Negroes steadfastly maintained their innocence. Bradley wanted a conviction and made a deal with Hughson to get it. If the tavern keeper backed Wilson's story about the "hatful of coins," Bradley would not prosecute him, especially since a search of the White Rose had uncovered nothing to link Hughson with the Hogg robbery. Hughson eagerly complied. Yes, he had seen the accused men in his place with a "hatful of coins" which they had squandered on drinks. Yes, he remembered how they had bragged about "easy money;" yes, anything the Attorney General wished him to say, he would say. Anything. At last, Bradley was satisfied. He kept his word; Hughson was set free and went jubilantly home to his slatternly wife, Elizabeth, and his homely, dull-witted, twenty-year-old daughter, Sara.

That night a noisy celebration rocked the White Rose Tavern. The barroom was crowded. All New York's underworld turned out to welcome Hughson back. Toothless harridans cackled over glasses of cheap rum. There were cutthroats and sneakthieves, harlots, procurers, and muggers—criminals of every sort and degree. All night long they drank and brawled.

Hughson, a thickset man, with bushy brows drawn over small, deep-set eyes, had a brutal face. He stood watching, huge hairy arms folded across his barrel chest.

Sara Hughson looked on with lacklustre eyes. She was a stupid, graceless girl without mental or physical charm. Mrs. Hughson stood by her husband, her lank, graying hair hanging to her shoulders in greasy strands. She had a thin, sallow face with ferret eyes. The Hughsons were an un-wholesome family, but this night they held court.

The revelry became an orgy. The air stank of stale to-bacco, rotgut whisky, and the sweat of many unwashed bodies. Despite the intense cold out-of-doors, the barroom was stifling and hot. Yet no one minded the discomfort or the stench. Johnny Hughson was giving drinks on the house. All had gone well for him. The constables never would find where he had hidden the loot. A pretty penny it was going to bring when he sold the silver and linens to the dealer from Philadelphia, who was coming to buy the lot. And he and the thief also had a handsome sum of money to share—nearly two hundred pounds sterling had been stolen from the tobacconist.

Perhaps in his exultation Hughson gave a fleeting thought to Prince and Caesar, whom he had doomed by his lies. Hughson knew they never had stolen a farthing from anyone. But it had been his neck or theirs—and Johnny Hughson wasn't going to dance on air at the end of a rope.

The thief, a slave named Pompey, owned by Johannes Vaarck, a baker, had worked with Hughson for several years, and the law never before had come so close. This time, Pompey had stirred up a storm by striking the Jew's wife. In the past, Hughson had warned him never to use violence against a white person, but Pompey had a vicious streak and had beaten up several robbery victims.

This fondness for using his fists was the slave's only defect as a partner in crime. In his daily routine, Pompey was a docile, willing worker, quick to learn and eager to please his master. Vaarck was well satisfied with him, for Pompey had become a skilled baker and worked side by side with his owner. The slave's conduct was beyond reproach; no one ever had seen him in such places as the White Rose; he never drank, gambled, or caroused. Pompey would be the last Negro in New York anyone would suspect of a crime.

He and Hughson made a good team. Pompey did the stealing and the tavern owner got rid of the loot through his Philadelphia contact. Now, unhappily, they'd have to lay low for a time until things cooled off.

The night patrol had been tripled since the incidents at the Hogg and Cohen places. Some rich men hired armed guards to watch their homes at night. However, Hughson knew that this state of alarm was only temporary. Once Prince and Caesar were executed, affairs would return to normal and Pompey could get busy again. In the meantime, there was a party to be enjoyed. Hughson poured himself a beaker of ale—none of the rotgut whisky or miserable rum for him.

He raised his glass high. "Here's to the law!" he cried and gulped the drink amid raucous laughter and hoarse cheers . . .

TWO

Hughson's well-being would undoubtedly have been shaken had he known of the unlikely enemy plotting his downfall. That person was Mary Burton, an obscure indentured servant. The pinch-faced, sixteen-year-old girl had been shipped to New York from the Dublin orphanage in which she was raised. In her entire life, Mary never had known a home, love, security, or comfort. Indentured to Hughson in 1739 for a seven-year period, Mary did all the unsavory chores at the White Rose. She made beds, did the laundry, tended fires, cleaned spitoons, scrubbed floors, worked in the kitchen, served drinks, waited on tables, and handled any other odd job that came along.

She worked seven days a week from dawn until late at night, ate slops, wore rags, and slept on a straw pallet in an airless alcove behind the kitchen. The Hughsons treated her as they would a stray cur; she was kicked, cuffed, and punched at will. No one in the family thought of her as anything but a human beast of burden.

The girl was quite homely with her mottled complexion, lumpy nose, slack mouth, and receding chin. Her long matted hair was the color of the dirty straw upon which she slept. She had black eyes that danced furtively back and forth. Mary detested the Hughsons. Often while sweating over some irksome task she plotted revenge against her master and his family. She vowed that one day she would even the score for all the degradation suffered at the hands of the Hughsons. Yes, she'd pay back all the others who had mistreated her as well. Even the slaves who frequented the White Rose mocked and humiliated her.

Oh, but there would come a time when she'd make them squirm. Alone, in the dark, on her pallet, she lay awake, scheming against her tormentors. But her visions of vengeance remained mere dreams. There were few opportunities for people such as Mary Burton to strike back. To Mary, everyone was an enemy. Perhaps the accumulation of hatred twisted her mind; she became obsessed with revenge.

Outwardly, Mary showed no sign that she harbored such dark thoughts, or any thoughts at all, for that matter. She remained as she had been, a drab, downtrodden drudge, passively carrying out her menial chores.

Mary knew her moment had arrived when Hughson was arrested as the fence in the Hogg case. She watched the constables poking about the tavern in search of the loot and contained her laughter. She knew where it was hidden. But rather than blurt out this secret, Mary remained mute. It amused her that the officers were digging and probing without success. For once, she had a feeling of power; there would be time enough to display it. Simply gloating over her chance to make Hughson suffer was satisfaction enough.

Everyone had underestimated Mary. She was ignorant but not stupid. Mary had spied on Hughson the night he buried the Hogg loot under the flooring of the tavern stable. She had watched him working by the light of a bull's-eye lantern, lifting up floor boards and replacing them so carefully that no clue remained to give away what had been done.

At first, Mary had wanted to tell the constables immediately, but that would have ruined her game. She could afford to wait a bit. It mattered nothing to her that Prince and Caesar were entirely innocent. They often had laughed at Mary. They could swing from the gibbet for all she cared. But she'd make certain that the Hughsons had their necks stretched, too.

Mary remained in the shadows during the homecoming party for the tavern keeper and observed the roistering and the carousing. She studied Hughson, noting his hearty good humor. She heard his laughter, even though the sound of his voice literally made her sick. She saw Elizabeth Hughson, that graying harridan, and her gaze fell on Sara, standing to one side, staring blankly at the partymakers.

Laugh, drink, raise the roof, the lot of you, Mary thought. You'll shed tears soon. The knife's at your throats and I'll be the one to draw it across your windpipes. Me. Mary Burton. The alley cat. You'll kick me no more. The jig's up, John Hughson.

Mary stood in the shadows and watched the revelers. Thinking of what was in store for them, she started to giggle with delight . . .

THREE

The pattern of Mary Burton's revenge began to unfold on the Sunday morning after the party when she awakened at daybreak as usual. The tavern was quiet except for the rasping snores from the upstairs bedrooms where the Hughsons slept off the effects of the merrymaking.

41

Also asleep in her room, over the tavern was a twenty-four-year-old woman named Peggy Kerry, who lived at the White Rose. Peggy's reputation was unsavory. Involved in petty thefts, she was also a well-known prostitute. However, of all the tavern's habitués, only Peggy Kerry ever had shown Mary the least kindness. Once she had given her a dress, another time a pair of shoes. She always had a smile or a friendly word for Mary. Despite this, the girl hated Peggy, who was shapely and pretty, the favorite of the tavern's male customers. It irked Mary that Peggy laughed and flirted with the men. She choked with envy. Men never smiled at her as they did at Peggy. Mary had known only sneers, taunts, and derision from men. And so she hated Peggy Kerry with a special venom. When the gallows trap dropped for the Hughsons, Mary would make certain that a noose would be around Peggy's slender neck as well.

Picking her way through the clutter and debris of the previous night—empty bottles, half eaten sausages, broken glasses, overturned tables—Mary went out into the morning. It was another bitter day. The snow was crunchy underfoot, but the fresh and crisp air was welcome after the foulness inside the tavern.

Mary waited on the stoop for a long time until a fat woman appeared, waddling slowly on the snowy walk. As she approached, Mary called, "Good day to you, Mrs. Hicks. And do you be on your way to church this early?"

Mrs. Hicks disdainfully turned her head. The likes of such trash speaking to her! She, who was the wife of Jethro Hicks, a constable and a man of importance. Rebecca

Hicks started to walk haughtily by, but Mary blocked the way.

"Slowly, slowly, me lady. You'd best not be running until you hear me out," Mary said.

The fat woman stared at the girl. "Why, you—you, slattern! Don't dare use that tone to me! I'll report you to the constable!" Rebecca croaked.

Mary made a mock curtsy. "Sorry, me lady. I'd be delighted, seeing as I have something to tell him of the Hogg robbery."

Rebecca's expression changed to suspicion. "And what would you know?" Mrs. Hicks asked contemptuously.

"I've word for the constable about Hogg, and if you don't tell him to come around at once, I'll sing to another constable. I'm thinking your mister won't be wanting another to win the glory, now would he?"

Mrs. Hicks spluttered, glared, turned around, and hurried home, muttering to herself. Mary looked after her, chuckling. She had planted the seed and knew it would take root that gray morning. She re-entered the tavern, wrinkling her nose in displeasure at the grating snores of the sleepers upstairs.

Then, as though nothing was awry, she set to work cleaning up the barroom. She collected mugs and washed them; she swept and scrubbed the littered floor and made the place passably neat. Having done this, she lit the kitchen fire and started breakfast—gruel, hoecakes, and coffee—but had barely begun when Constable Hicks stormed into the White Rose.

43

He was a big man, over six feet tall, wide-shouldered and muscular. His face was hawklike: curved nose, thin lips framing a sternly set mouth, a pointed chin.

Mary swung around as the constable stomped into the kitchen. His eyes burned into hers. For an instant she almost fainted from fright. Hicks leveled a thick finger at her, aiming it like a pistol.

"Now then, wench! What's all this?" he snapped. "You'd best be damned sure I've not broken the Sabbath to go off on a wild-goose chase! I'd not take to it kindly!"

Mary's knees shook. She hung onto the edge of a table to steady herself. Trying to speak, she could not utter a sound. She was thoroughly afraid of Hicks; what had seemed so simple to do only a little while earlier now seemed impossible. The constable stepped closer to her; pinpoints of icy light danced in his cruel eyes. Mary could see the smallpox pits and scars that marred his face.

"Well, speak up wench!" Hicks ordered. He cuffed her with such force that she fell to her knees. "Maybe that'll loosen your tongue. Now talk, damn your hide!"

Mary pulled herself erect. She touched the bruised cheek with work-roughened fingertips. Tears burned in her eyes. Hicks raised his huge, calloused hand again and she cried out, "No! Don't sir, please! I'll tell you! It's Hughson has the Hogg loot!"

"What? We searched this place from top to bottom—"

"Ah, sir, but it's hidden under the stable flooring."

Suddenly Hicks reached and grabbed a fistful of her

44

hair. He yanked so hard that she yelped in pain. "You're a damned liar!" he growled.

"Oh, no! No, sir! It's God's truth!"

He thrust the girl roughly aside. "Maybe. We never thought to look there." Once again the thick forefinger jabbed the air. "You keep mum and go about your work. I'll bring back more men. Remember. Not a word, or I'll tear out your tongue." He turned and strode out.

After Hicks left, Mary slumped weakly onto a kitchen stool and wept for a few minutes; even her moment of triumph had been spoiled. That hurt her more than Hicks' blow. She had expected different treatment from the constable; after all, wasn't she doing him a favor? This only proved that every hand was turned against her.

A shout from upstairs snapped her to attention. She daubed at the tears with the corner of her soiled apron as Hughson bellowed, "Mary! Damn your soul, Mary! I'm raging with hunger! Fetch some breakfast! Mary! Answer me, damn you!"

"Aye, Mr. Hughson," the girl called. "I'll have it in a jiffy!" Hughson mumbled some reply. She heard the door of his bedroom slam shut. Mary poked up the fire, and when the flames leaped merrily upward, she murmured, "This is the last breakfast I'll be preparing for you, me lordship. The last!"

As she prepared the meal, the rest of the family—mother and daughter—screeched for their breakfasts, and Peggy Kerry also called down. Mary took a tray to each.

45

Since no other lodgers were in the tavern, she had time to enjoy a mug of coffee. While she was sipping the brew, a nearby church-steeple clock tolled eight times. The last stroke was still reverberating when Hicks returned accompanied by two constables, who carried crowbars and shovels.

"All right, wench, show us the loot," Hicks said.

Mary gulped the coffee, wiped her mouth with the back of a reddened hand, and went to him.

"This way," she said . . .

FOUR

For the first time in her life, Mary felt like somebody. After Hicks and his fellow constables had uncovered the loot, Hughson, his wife, Sara, and Peggy Kerry were arrested. The women wept and pleaded, swearing they knew nothing about the theft or the stolen goods, which was quite true. Hughson had not confided his side business to them.

The tavern keeper had blustered, threatened, and cursed, but all his storming and railing made no impression on Hicks. The constable had wavered briefly only when Hughson offered to split the money he would get for the goods. However, the fear of being exposed outweighed monetary gain, and Hicks ordered the prisoners taken to City Prison, where they were locked up in cells adjoining those of Prince and Caesar.

Watching her master being taken away, Mary could

not resist taunting him. She stood by the tavern door, and as Hughson passed, curtsied demurely and said, "It was me what peached, sir. I want you to know that. May you burn in hell!"

Hughson stopped in his tracks. His ruddy face paled as he stared incredulously at her. "You! To be done in by you!" He shouted. He lunged at her, but was slammed back against the door jamb by a blow from a constable's truncheon. The officer raised the weapon menacingly. "Try that again, me bucko, and I'll stave in your skull! Move on, now."

Propelled by a push from the constable, Hughson stumbled down the steps. His wife and Sara followed, eyes red and swollen, clothing awry, hair disheveled. They were pitiful and wretched creatures, overwhelmed by what had happened. Peggy Kerry moved by gracefully. Even with manacled hands she carried herself with a touch of dignity that belied her social position and the present situation.

As she brushed past Mary, Peggy whispered, "Why? Why me?"

Mary flushed and lowered her eyes, momentarily touched by a shred of shame. There had been no reason to betray Peggy. But it was too late for regrets. Peggy went out into the street and the procession moved off with Hicks bringing up the rear, a gunny sack filled with the stolen goods slung over his shoulder. He beckoned to Mary. "You come along, too, lass. They'll be wanting your testimony," he said.

She nodded and trudged on by the big constable's side, aware of people at windows staring after the file of prisoners and their captors.

After locking up the Hughsons and Peggy Kerry, Hicks took Mary to the prison office. She was awed by the fine gentlemen gathered there; these were truly the "people in ruffles"—elegant, well-groomed men in fine clothes and powdered wigs, gentry such as Mary had seen only from afar. She hesitated timidly on the threshold, aware of her soiled dress, dust-streaked face, and untidy hair.

She belonged in the scullery of a low tavern on Vesey Street, not with such lordly personages. Had a chance come for her to run, she would have fled. But Hicks clamped his great hand around her wrist and drew her inside.

A voice boomed, "Ah, here's Constable Hicks, and this must be the lass who broke this case for us."

The men gathered around her. She heard names—Judge Daniel Horsmanden, Judge Frederick Philipse, Mr. Robert Murray, Judge John Chambers, Attorney General Richard Bradley. The high and the mighty of New York City. She stood dumbly, trying to smile, feeling giddy, fearful of collapsing in their presence.

Judge Horsmanden was a tall, spare man, with a seamy, deeply lined face and cold blue eyes magnified by square-lensed spectacles perched on the tip of his long nose. He fancied himself a philanthropist. With his wife, Horsmanden had organized a welfare committee to aid the city's "poor and unfortunate inhabitants . . . who have

48

suffered such hardships and misery during the past difficult winter. . . ."

He decided on the spot that something must be done for Mary. The girl could not return to Hughson's "foul den of iniquity." But she had no place to go and no friends or relatives in New York. The Judge suddenly remembered that his wife needed a scullery maid. Mary could have the job if she wanted it; all he had to do was transfer her indenture from Hughson to himself.

Calling the girl aside, he told her what was in his mind. Hardly believing her good fortune, she accepted with alacrity. Much had happened to her in a short time. Only yesterday she had been hopelessly trapped in a morass. She happily accompanied the Judge to his home, a splendid mansion on Pearl Street.

Mary stared wide-eyed at the rosewood furniture, the chandeliers, mirrors, Oriental rugs, and gleaming crystal glass. Never in her life had she seen such luxury. Surely, she thought, not even the King lived in such splendor. And this was to be her home. How far away the squalor of the White Rose seemed now.

The girl was turned over to the housekeeper, a tall, haughty Negress named Cordelia. With ill-concealed distaste, the housekeeper led her up to an attic room—a mere cubbyhole barely large enough for a bed, a small table, and a chair. To Mary it seemed like the grand ballroom of a royal palace. She could not remember ever having slept in a bed; at the orphanage, she had had only a wooden bunk, and in the White Rose, a straw pallet.

Cordelia then led Mary down the back stairs to the servants' washhouse. She ordered a pair of slave boys to fill a large oaken washtub with steaming water. When they had finished, Cordelia shooed the boys off, made Mary shed the rags she wore and climb into the tub. Despite the girl's protests, the housekeeper scrubbed her vigorously with a stiff brush and strong soap.

Mary screeched and yowled as the hard bristles raked her skin, but Cordelia rubbed away as though washing soiled laundry. At last she handed Mary a rough towel, and when the girl had dried herself, gave her clean clothes and a pair of work shoes.

Freshly attired, hair brushed, cheeks gleaming, Mary looked presentable. Cordelia eyed her critically: "You ain't no beauty, but we can't make a silk purse out'n a sow's ear. Now then. It's off to the scullery for you."

The kitchen was presided over by a slave named Joanna, a prepossessing woman who at once put Mary to work shelling peas, peeling potatoes, washing pots and pans. A person unused to hard labor would have been incapable of coping with the many chores Joanna piled on Mary, but compared to the daily routine at the White Rose, this was easy.

Mary toiled cheerfully away. Joanna was a hard, demanding taskmaster, but a fair one. She spared neither herself nor the kitchen staff—an assistant cook, a baker, and the two boys who had poured Mary's bath water. In all, Horsmanden owned ten slaves. He also had a white

bondsman gardener and a coachman named Cato, a huge
Negro who wore an elaborate livery of scarlet, with gold
braid and epaulets. Heads turned when the Horsmanden
carriage, drawn by four matched grays, rolled past.

Everything about Horsmanden was impressive—his
wife, Eleanor, who carried herself like a grand duchess, his
house, furnishings, and garden. Daniel Horsmanden had
wealth and position; he epitomized the rich of New York
City.

People such as the Judge led the good life and wanted
nothing changed or disturbed; as long as all went smooth-
ly, they were courteous, generous, and amiable. It would
have been unthinkable for Horsmanden to treat an under-
ling—even a slave—with rudeness. But this well-mannered
deportment was only a veneer. Should the *status quo* be
even slightly threatened, this urbane man and others like
him dropped their civilized façade and showed their un-
derlying ruthlessness.

A slave who committed a minor offense was flogged at
his master's orders. If he died under the lash, there was
neither guilt or remorse. The only value given a slave was
a financial one. Horsmanden and his kind willingly accepted the monetary loss when it became necessary to discipline a slave. Not only slaves, but also the poverty-stricken
white bondsmen were treated with equal ferocity if they
appeared to menace the social order. The rich fancied
themselves encircled by enemies who prowled like wolf
packs waiting to pounce at the first hint of weakness. The
terrible winter had sharpened the rift between the classes

51

as hunger, cold, and physical discomfort added to the ever present discontent. When Mary Burton denounced the Hughsons and Peggy Kerry, even the most unfeeling sensed the unrest stirring in the city.

It seemed beyond comprehension that an ignorant sixteen-year-old such as Mary could touch off the powder keg, yet only a short time afterward, she created a condition that all but paralyzed the city, took nearly a hundred lives, and loosed a state of hysteria that raged unchecked for weeks. All this came only after Mary realized that she possessed a power which fed on fear—a power she used to whip up a frenzy unparalleled since the infamous Salem Witch Trials of 1692. A similarly lurid drama would soon be enacted in New York—a spectacle of mass horror played out by human marionettes, with Mary Burton as the un-likely puppetmaster pulling the strings.

FIVE

Before the curtain was raised on the main attraction, a side show was enacted, a minor prelude to the all-star performance. The morning after Hughson's arrest, Johannes Vaarck, Pompey's master, informed the authorities that the slave had run away during the night. Titus Mills, the sheriff, immediately notified a volunteer group known as the "slave catchers." These men were specialists in tracking down runaway slaves with their highly trained bloodhounds. A fugitive slave's owner always paid a handsome reward if his property was returned alive and unharmed. It was a profitable business for the slave catchers.

The dogs soon picked up Pompey's trail. He had followed the expected route, heading north through the woods, hoping to hide out in the wilderness and elude capture until he could join up with friendly Indians, who always offered runaway Negroes a sanctuary. The slave catchers kept after Pompey with implacable determination, and he was quickly cornered. Instead of meekly surrendering, as did most runaways, he put up a fight during which a white man was stabbed to death.

Now, Pompey was not only a fugitive but also a killer. He would have been flogged for running off; certain execution faced him for slaying a white. Pompey had fled after Hughson's arrest, certain that the tavern keeper would betray him. Once Hughson talked, the hangman's noose awaited Pompey; his only hope lay in escape, but that road was closed. Nothing remained for him except the gallows or, perhaps, slow, fiery death at the stake. He refused to take either alternative.

As the slave catchers closed in, ". . . the Black faced us, lips drawn in a ferocious snarl like an animal at bay. The hunting knife glinted in his fist, already crimsoned by our comrade's blood. . . . With a defiant shout, he plunged the blade into his heart and fell dead at our feet. . . . He had cheated us of our bounty money," one of his pursuers later wrote.

Johannes Vaarck flew into a rage when Pompey's corpse was brought in. He had lost a skilled and valuable slave who would be difficult to replace. Even worse, the baker could not understand why Pompey had run off. He seldom punished the man and allowed him privileges few other slaves enjoyed. Other slaveowners had warned Vaarck that he was "too easy" with Pompey and would one day regret his leniency. The way things had turned out, he probably should have heeded their advice. Still, he was not sorry for having treated Pompey fairly and kept wondering why the slave had betrayed his trust.

The only person in the city with the answer remained silent in his prison cell. John Hughson knew there was no point in revealing the criminal role Pompey had played. He could gain nothing by making charges against a dead man. Thanks to him, the authorities already had Prince and Caesar; they needed no additional culprits—at least culprits who could not be hanged.

The tavern keeper was resigned to his fate. He had no qualms that innocent persons would be executed with him. A full confession of his sole guilt might spare them, but Hughson was not a man to make noble gestures.

He cared nothing about Prince and Caesar—two Blacks more or less didn't matter. And why shield his wife—the nagging shrew had made his life miserable for years. Sara? That dull, ugly clod. She'd be better off dead. At least she'd never again have to face sneers and insults. Peggy Kerry? Good riddance! Soon enough, pretty Peggy would sin no more.

An attempted escape by a slave always aroused a furor. Slaveowners bustled about nervously checking the security over their own bondsmen. Armed guards patrolled slave quarters, and a sharp watch was kept on house servants. Men kept loaded pistols at hand; women and girls stayed close to home. And rumors of real trouble brewing among the Negroes were on everyone's tongue.

Adding to the tension were unconfirmed reports of Spanish men-of-war sighted at various points along the coast. The sea war with Spain was getting worse; there had been several clashes between British and Spanish vessels. People's anxieties were raised when New York's Governor Clarke made public a letter from Governor James Oglethorpe of Georgia, which stated in part:

> "I wish to pass on to Your Excellency some intelligence I have had of a villainous design by the enemy. . . . The Spaniards have employed emissaries to burn all towns in English North America . . . and for that purpose are using priests disguised as physicians, teachers, fencing masters, and the like. . . ."

For years, Oglethorpe had been harassed by Spanish raiding parties from Florida, across the Georgia border. Spaniards made friends of slaves and Indians, inciting them to revolt against the English. Driven to distraction by such forays, Oglethorpe imagined that there was a widespread Spanish conspiracy to destroy all the English colonies. He raised once more the long dormant cry of a "papist plot."

Plagued by numerous difficulties, brooding over his military failures since the beginning of the war against the

Spanish in 1739, Oglethorpe bombarded his fellow colony governors with letters cautioning them about alleged Spanish plots and plotters. Oglethorpe was driven by bigotry and frustration, not by facts and logic. "The good governor of Georgia sees a Spaniard under every bush and a papist conspirator in every shadow. He is well-intentioned, I presume, but a trifle unbalanced," one high-ranking officer said of Oglethorpe. It was an opinion that was fairly widespread.

However, the Governor of Georgia found support in New York City. Animosity there against Spanish Catholics and Catholics in general was quite strong. A law that decreed death for any Catholic priest who dared enter the province had been on the books since 1700. The same statute forbade "the practising or teaching of popish prayers, granting absolution, hearing confession, saying the mass or any popish ceremonies. . . ."

Oglethorpe's letter worried New Yorkers, for there were a number of Spaniards in the city. In April, 1740, a British privateer had seized an enemy merchantman, taking the ship as a prize and making the crew prisoners of war. Among the captives were nineteen Negroes and mulattoes from Brazil, where they had been freemen. However, in English colonies slavery was based on a man's color and not his previous station in life. The Spanish colored men were therefore adjudged slaves and put up for sale at auction. Despite the seamen's protests that they were free and not slaves, the sale was held. Antonio de San Bendido became De Lancey's Antonio; Antonio de la Cruz was renamed Mesnard's Antonio; Juan de la Sylva was called Lacey's Juan or Wan, after his new master.

The Spanish slaves swore to escape from bondage and take vengeance on those who had enslaved them. Juan de la Sylva openly declared, "I shall yet wash my hands in the blood of my so-called master!"

De la Sylva was flogged for making this utterance. His militant comrades also felt the lash many times, but the whippings failed to break their spirits. Instead, the beatings aroused even greater resentment and defiance among them.

From time to time, their numbers increased as English privateers and warships brought in more prizes and prisoners. By March, 1741, some hundred dark-skinned Spanish subjects had been sold at the Slave Market.

The presence of these desperate men served to increase the apprehensions of New Yorkers. Any breach of discipline by the Spanish Negroes was exaggerated until it became a full-scale mutiny. People agitated to get them out of the city, but nothing came of it. De Lancey, Mesnard, and the other prominent people who had purchased Spaniards would not give up their bondsmen. Indeed, it was a mark of status to own one or more of them. Paradoxically, the Spaniards were good, conscientious workers, in spite of their rebellious attitudes.

As one merchant who owned a Spaniard said, "I can't turn my back on the villain less he slip a knife between my ribs, but I can depend on him to do a day's work. . . ."

Undoubtedly the Spaniards were a potential danger,

but they had caused no real trouble since their arrival. However, if Oglethorpe's letter were true and disguised priests bent on arson actually were sneaking into the city, the Spanish slaves posed a major threat.

Nobody, least of all Governor Clarke, could offer any sound reasons for making public the Oglethorpe missive. "Have we not been sufficiently afflicted these past months?" a saddlemaker wrote his brother in Boston. "The drought, the cruel winter, the fear of a slave uprising have been staggering burdens. And now this thing to fret about. I have always been chary of the Spanish Blacks. They are a mean and murderous looking lot, papists to the core. These are hard days indeed. . . ."

Oglethorpe's words aroused so much consternation that Governor Clarke felt compelled to counteract them. He issued a statement intended to reassure New Yorkers, saying:

> "The possibility of papists infiltrating this city must not be embroidered. . . . We are maintaining a diligent vigil against an invasion by such miscreants. However, they are infernally clever and we therefore urge all loyal men to beware of strangers. . . . We shall root out these incendiaries and enemies of the only true faith. . . ."

Clarke's clumsy pronouncement was interpreted as an admission that Spanish agents already had penetrated the city. It brought such a feverish reaction that the Governor urged something be done to divert the people's attention.

Attorney General Richard Bradley promptly obliged him by bringing to trial Prince and Caesar, the slaves accused of committing the Hogg and Cohen robberies. The case proceeded with Judge Daniel Horsmanden on the bench. Since slaves had no right to a jury trial, there was no jury.

Bradley merely read into the record the deposition of the sailor, Christopher Wilson, who originally had accused the Negroes. Even though John Hughson was currently awaiting trial, his deposition also was admitted. The two slaves sat numbly in court, barely understanding the procedures. Both showed visible effects of their stay in jail. Thin and haggard, their faces were marked by bruises and welts of many beatings.

The trial lasted scarcely twenty minutes. A lawyer appointed by the court to defend the slaves halfheartedly asked the Judge for clemency, but Horsmanden was dispensing none that day. He found both men guilty and sentenced them to be hanged in chains on Collect Island, ". . . there to be exposed on the gallows in open view until flesh molders from bone. . . ."

An opportunity was afforded Judge Frederick Philipse, owner of the slaves, to petition the court for mercy. Except in cases where a slave was charged with manslaughter, murder, or rape, the master usually requested that his bondsman's life be spared so that the slaveowner would incur no financial loss. Since one of the defendants allegedly had struck a white woman, Philipse refused to intercede. "I shall not raise my voice in defense of a creature so debased as to perpetrate such a bestial deed. It matters not that I shall be out of pocket and have to replace these slaves. Far better that justice be served!"

SIX

The men were hanged a few days later. As always at public executions, a large crowd watched. Rowboats and skiffs dotted the waters of The Collect. Everyone was in a festive mood. Children dashed about flinging snowballs and rolling in the snowdrifts. Although the sun shone brightly, the day was cold that mid-March morning. Peddlers selling hot drinks and butter cakes did a good business.

The spectators cheered and applauded when the public hangman, wearing the traditional black hood and robe, took up his post beside the gallows, ready to spring the trap. The victims, their legs in irons and their hands manacled behind them, were shoved unceremoniously up the scaffold steps.

As the noose was being adjusted around his neck, Caesar screamed, in a voice that carried across the water to the crowd, "I done nothin'! I done nothin'! Please, Master, let me live!" Prince submitted to the noose without a word. The trap dropped open.

The spectators departed reluctantly but well satisfied. It had been a fine hanging, and many turned for another look at the bodies. A band of youths mocked Caesar's last cry. "I done nothin'! I done nothin'!" one of the young men shrieked as his companions doubled over with laughter.

Knots of sullen-eyed slaves gathered to stare at the festive whites returning from the executions. The coachmen driving rich men's carriages did not conceal their hatred, but glared at the homegoers. The slaves said nothing; their silence held more menace than shouted curses.

A visitor from the city of Albany, marking the air of hostility shown by the Negroes, wrote in his diary:

> "Today a hanging took place. Two Blacks for stealing. I tried to watch but such sights sicken me. The New York City folk enjoyed this grisly sight & flocked to see the executions behaving as though at a carnival. . . . The Blacks here harbor murderous thoughts. One feels their anger. I should not be surprised if one day they rise up. I shall be glad to leave this city and return home. . . . There is much in this place that makes me apprehensive. . . ."

Mary Burton had been in the crowd at the shores of The Collect. Young men, clowning in the snow, flirted with other girls, but never gave Mary a second look. She pretended indifference at being ignored, but inwardly, secretly, envied the carefree youths and girls having such a good time.

But that was soon forgotten. Perched on a snow-covered rock, Mary strained her eyes to see the activities on the island. This was her first public execution, and although she was aware that Prince and Caesar were entirely innocent, she felt no pity for them. Soon she'd be standing in this very place to watch the hangman finish off the Hughsons and Peggy Kerry. She looked forward to the day. And before that she would speak out to the men on the grand jury and they would listen gravely to a nobody like her. Ah, the whole city would know Mary Burton, and those same lads who stared straight through her today would take notice of her. Mary Burton would soon have her day in the sun.

Mary stayed on long after the crowds departed. She stared at the bodies, unable to explain her fascination with the gallows. At last she trudged slowly back to the Horsmanden house, reporting to the kitchen very late. Joanna scolded her, and when Mary answered defiantly, the cook became furious.

"Don't sass me, missy. You do your work proper or I'll have you put to the whip! There's pots to scour! I want them scoured now!" Joanna shouted.

Taken aback by the cook's fury, Mary got busy at once. She seethed with outraged anger. This was the sort of treatment she'd had at the White Rose; she was still at the bottom of the pile, stepped on even by a Black. She was lower than a slave. Sweat poured down her face as she cleaned and shined the huge copper pots. A single purpose possessed her. Revenge. She'd scheme forever, every day of her life, finding a way to get even.

Mary did not have to wait very long. Her fantasy became a reality in an unexpected and unlikely way. During the night of Saturday, March 18, a sentry walking his post on the Battery seawall noticed flames licking at the roof of the Governor's House. He roused the garrison, and men tumbled out of bed as the fire bells began clanging. Fanned by a strong wind coming in from the Bay, the fire spread to several adjoining buildings. Alarm bells sounded all over the city, and volunteer fire companies, dragging water wagons and hose carts, raced to fight the blaze. By the time the flames had been put out, the Governor's House, a section of the barracks, an arsenal building, and some residences were badly damaged.

An investigation on March 19 showed that tinsmiths, who had been repairing drainpipes on the Governor's House, had carelessly started the fire. It had smoldered for hours under the eaves until discovered. The blaze aroused no suspicion until the Fort George Sergeant-at-Arms reported a dozen muskets, bayonets, powder and ball missing from a supply room. Apparently the place had been forcibly entered while attention was centered on the fire.

When the theft of the guns became known, men wondered if the fire had been an accident or had been started deliberately to cover the theft of the weapons. On the other hand, perhaps someone simply had taken advantage of the situation to steal the arms. The chief worry gnawing at everyone was who had stolen the weapons and for what purpose. During the following week, the fire at the Governor's House and the missing muskets held the city's attention. Then, on Saturday, March 25, a fire was discovered in a private home on William Street.

At 1:00 A.M. the cry "Fire!" echoed through the sleep-

Fort George as seen from across the river. *Eno Collection.*

ing city. Black smoke was seen rolling from the rear of a Georgian house owned by Captain Isiah Randall, a retired shipmaster. An alert volunteer fire company confined the conflagration to the kitchen and put out the flames.

The Randall fire would have been written off as routine but for two unusual factors. The first was that money, a watch, and some jewelry had been stolen from the burning house. The second, and more alarming, was a fireman's discovery of oil-soaked cotton waste in the charred kitchen.

Robbery and arson made a frightening combination. The theft could be explained away; it was known that volunteer fire companies often included some of the city's roughest residents. Light-fingered firemen occasionally had rifled a home while extinguishing the flames. The oil-soaked cotton waste was another matter; it smacked of arson. The next day, a Sunday, the fear of arson increased when a stableman in the Fly Mart found a pan of glowing coals concealed in his hayloft. Had he missed it, a devastating fire might have resulted. Now consternation began spreading through the city. Apparently a gang of arsonists and thieves was at large in New York.

Within the next few days a whole rash of fires broke out, one after the other. At midday, a John Street warehouse burst into flames. Someone reported having seen a Negro leap from the ground floor and run away. Several hours later, a large cornshed went up in smoke. Even as firemen battled that blaze, bells pealed for another, a few blocks away. Among the crowd that gathered was a slave named Quack, who was overheard muttering, "Burn them! Burn them! That's what they understand!" Quack stumbled away, "shaking his head and laughing delightedly," according to an eyewitness who reported the incident to a constable.

Quack was arrested as an arsonist although known to be mentally backward and given to uttering foolish statements. Soon after Quack's arrest, a slave named Cuffee got into an argument with another Negro. Words led to blows, and the men fought. Cuffee beat up the other slave, who vowed to "set things right." The man told the authorities that Cuffee was the one who had jumped out of the John Street warehouse after setting it afire. Constables promptly put Cuffee under arrest.

After Cuffee had been locked up in a cell, Attorney General Bradley remembered that the slave was a troublemaker. During the recent "Hard Winter" Cuffee had been flogged for stating, "Some people have too much and others too little. My master has a lot of money. But pretty soon he's going to lose it and I'll be rich!" Such talk by a slave was considered seditious, and Cuffee received forty lashes for making "inflammatory remarks."

If the authorities had expected the arrests of Quack and Cuffee to end the fires, they were disappointed. During the first week of April there were a dozen fires. Arson was apparent in almost every case—hot coals covered with straw, oil-soaked rags stuffed in corners, slow-burning matches dropped on inflammable materials were found.

Fire fighting in the eighteenth century. *I. N. Phelps Stokes Collection of American Historical Prints.*

Looting was widespread; something of value was stolen each time the alarm bells sounded.

The fires followed no set pattern. They broke out during the day and at night. No section of the city was spared. The Governor's House had been first, but less important homes, shops, storehouses, and farm buildings were also put to the torch. This fiery epidemic brought to mind the prophet in the Fly Mart, the year before, with his prediction of blood and fire, ashes and ruin. Again came whispers of Hagar's evil spells, and some claimed to have seen her ghost hovering about the ruins of the shack in which she had lived.

Far more ominous than mysterious strangers and ghostly apparitions was the rising insolence the slaves displayed as the fires became widespread. The Negroes knew their masters were frightened, and that pleased them. As the number of fires increased, the authorities began to believe that there was a Negro plot to burn the city. As an initial step to squelch such a plan the most militant Spanish Negroes were arrested and put in solitary confinement; no proof existed that the Spaniards were leading or planning to lead a Negro revolt, but they presented the most convenient scapegoats.

Once the Spaniards were locked up, Governor Clarke confidently announced, "The incarceration of these perfidious Spaniards will be followed by a period of tranquility and calm for us. . . ." The Governor's optimism soon turned to gloom. The fires continued, day after day, night after night, until it seemed to one New Yorker that, "We

68

shall be consumed by flame . . . there is no hope for us. . . ."

In desperation, Governor Clarke offered a reward of one hundred pounds sterling for information leading to the capture and conviction of those behind the conspiracy. To encourage potential informers, Clarke promised immunity from prosecution and a full pardon to anyone implicated in the plot if he came forward with facts.

Although no immediate claimants for the reward appeared, the Governor's overture had one beneficial effect. By the end of the second week in April, the fires and robberies came to an abrupt halt. For several days, the alarm bells did not toll even once. The city started assuming its normal routines.

There was a general belief that the arsonists had taken fright, fearful of betrayal by one of their own number to whom one hundred pounds might mean more than loyalty.

Clarke was overjoyed that the emergency appeared to have passed. Talk was heard that the Spanish Negroes would be released soon, while the charge of arson against Quack and Cuffee was to be dropped, since the evidence against them was so thin.

But the offer of a reward reaped an unexpected harvest that far outstripped Clarke's anticipations and briefly made a heroine of Mary Burton. This shabby Joan of Arc discovered a simple fact—that fear reduced even intelligent men to the level of a raving mob. She used this knowledge so craftily that, for a time, the scullery maid practi-

ture; but that on the contrary, Affiſtance is certainly given in an underhand Manner from *France*. How great ſoever, neverthelefs, ſuch Aids may be, People are perfuaded that *Spain* can never ſucceed unlefs *France* heartily joins her. According to all Appearance, *Great Britain* will not be eaſily prevail'd upon, as Affairs are circumſtanced, to hearken to any Terms of Accommodation, being ſenſible how ardently the Queen of *Spain* wiſhes for a Peace. If the Spaniards ſhould venture to undertake to paſs into *Italy*, Admiral Haddock would probably have an Opportunity of renewing the ſcene repreſented in the Year 1718, near *Syracuſe*. In the mean time both the Land and Sea Armies of *Spain* are in great Motion. Publick Miniſters in all the Courts of *Europe* are buſily employ'd in the moſt important Negociations, the Succeſs of which in a ſhort Time will be known.

A Report is current, that an Ambaſſador Extraordinary will ſoon arrive here from the Court of France, charged, as it is ſaid, with a plan for accommodating the Differences between this Court and that of Spain.

The Eaſt India Company will ſpeedily take into their Service three Ships of between three and four hundred Tons, which are to be employ'd in the Eaſt Indies againſt Angria the Pirate.

PHILADELPHIA, April 9.
Friday laſt arrived here a Spaniſh Snow laden with Wine, taken at Aruba, and ſent in by the George, Capt. Drummond, of this Port. She came from Teneriffe and had a Paſs from the Dutch Conſul, but no Dutchmen on board. On Account of this Paſs, the Governor of Curacoa, ſent out a Veſſel to demand the Prize of Capt. Drummond, but he refus'd to reſtore her, fir'd at the Dutchman and beat him off. Before the Taking of this Snow, Capt. Drummond had taking two Sloops, one was ſent into Jamaica and condemn'd there, the other being a good Sailor, he has fitted out for a Tender, with 30 Men, and Arms ſuitable, under the Command of Capt. Sibbald; ſhe is call'd the Victory. On the 16th of February, the George the Victory, and the Prize Snow, being in Company off Hiſpaniola, were chas'd by two Men of War, which they ſuppos'd to be Enemies; the George and Victory left the Prize, and ſhe was taken; but the Victory falling in with the Grand Engliſh Fleet two Days after, found they were Engliſh Men of War who had taken the Prize, and ſhe was reſtor'd to

Capt. Sibbald, by Order from Admiral Vernon. The Victory convoy'd her tho' the Windward Paſſage, and return'd to look out for the George, from whom ſhe Parted in the Chaſe.

By this Snow we have Letters from the Fleet of the 20th of February, adviſing that they were extended along the Coaſt of Hiſpaniola for the Conveniency of Wooding and Watering, that they had made a vaſt Number of Faſcines, and were to ſail in a Day or two, for ſome Spaniſh Port. That the French Fleet were gone home; and that a great Number of the Engliſh Soldiers were ſick, ſeveral of the Officers dead, &c.

NEW-YORK.

By the HONOURABLE.

George Clarke, Eſq; His Majeſty's Lieutenant Governour and Commander in Chief of the Province of *New York* and Territories thereon depending in *America*.

A PROCLAMATION.

WHEREAS ſeveral Houſes and other Buildings within the City of *New-York*, have frequently of late been ſecretly and moſt wickedly and maliciouſly ſet on Fire by divers wicked Perſons, to the great Damage of many, and the great Terror of all the Inhabitants within the ſaid City.

And whereas the Mayor, Aldermen and Commonalty of the ſaid City, purſuant to a late Order and Reſolution of that Board, have Requeſted me to Iſſue a Proclamation, offering ſuch Rewards to ſuch Perſons, and in ſuch Manner as in and by the ſame Order and Reſolution as herein after are expreſſed, for the Diſcovery of any Perſons or Perſon lately concerned in ſetting Fire to any Dwelling-Houſe Store-Houſe within the ſaid City,

I have Therefore in Purſuance of the ſaid Requeſt, by & with the conſent of His Majeſ. ty's Council for this *Province*, thought fit to Iſſue this Proclamation, hereby offering a Reward of *One Hundred Pounds* current Money of this Province, to any White Perſon that ſhall diſcover any Perſons or Perſon to have been lately concerned in ſetting Fire to any Dwelling-Houſe Store-Houſe or other Building within this City, if ſuch Perſons or Perſon ſo to be diſcovered, ſhall be convicted thereof; and that ſuch Perſon who ſhall make ſuch Diſcovery, as aforeſaid faid (being one of the Parties concerned in fetting Fire to any fuch Building, as aforefaid) fhall neverthelefs be pardoned for the fame. And if any Slave fhall make fuch Difcovery, as aforefaid, he fhall be Pardoned, and made free, and fhall alfo receive the Sum of *Twenty Pounds*, and the Mafter or Owner of fuch Slave fhall receive *Twenty Five Pounds*, in Confideration of his Slave's being made free, as aforefaid. And if any free Negro, Mullatto or Indian fhall make fuch Difcovery, as aforefaid, he fhall be pardoned, if concerned in fetting Fire to any fuch Building, as aforefaid, and fhall alfo have and receive *Forty Five Pounds*, for fuch his or her Difcovery, as aforefaid. All which Sums of Money above mentioned, the Mayor, Aldermen and Commonalty of the City of *New-York*, have in and by their faid Order, Refolution and Requeft undertaken fhall be duly paid, as Rewards to fuch Perfons, and in fuch manner as is above expreffed concerning the fame, and purfuant to their Order and Refolution above mentioned.

Given under my Hand and Seal at New York, this 17th Day of April, Anno Domini, 1741. and in the 14th Year of His Majefty's Reign.

By His Honour's Command,

George Clarke.

Geo. Jof. Moore, D. Cl. Council.

GOD Save the KING.

Extract of a Letter from *Jamaica*.

Kingfton, March 6, 1740.

—— This Day arrived here a Snow Man of War from *London*, who in her Paffage here, touch'd at *Antigoa*, but what Intelligence fhe brings, is to us ftill unknown. the Capt, not fuffering any of his People to come on Shore, nor any of the People of this Ifland to come on board of him, by which we imagine fhe has brought an Extraordinary Packet.

And that eight Tranfports with Convoy, fail'd hence, in which we have, furnifh'd, one Thoufand fenfible Negroes for the Ufe of the Expedition

This Afternoon we had feven Men arrived from *Carthagena*, who inform us, that they, and all the *Englifh* Prifoners were fet at Liberty, and that of the 3500 Men left there, there was not above 1500 alive, and that the Fleet had carry'd a great many of their Cannon away with them.

By Capt. *Betbell* from *Jamaica*. we hear that the brave Capt. *Warren* has taken two Prizes more, and that one of our Men of War has taken a French Man of War, who was Convoy to a large Fleet of Store Ships bound to *Cartbagena*, but parted from them in a Storm. The Admiral, however, has pofted fome Men of War in proper Places to interrupt them.

We have now certain Accounts of the *French* Fleet being gone home.

Laft Week His Honour the Governour was pleafed to Iffue a Proclamation, appointing *Wednefday* the 13th of May a general Faft.

This Morning arrived here Capt. *Seymour*, and Capt. *King* from *Jamaica* in 24 Days, but they bring us no News from the Fleet; on Account being recieved of Admiral *Vernon* fince our laft Advices from *Jamaica*, the particulars of which are confirm'd.

Laft Week there was a general Combination of the Bakers not to Bake, becaufe Wheat is at a high price, which occafioned fome Difturbance, and reduced fome, notwithftanding their Riches, to a fudden want of Bread.

Cuftom Houfe New York, Inward Entries.
Sloop *William* and *Mary*, W. *Beckman*, from *Bofton*, —— *Succefs*, T. *Smith*, —— *Mary and Sarah*, *Rich. Newbold* —— *Charming Joana*; J. *Righton*, from *Bermuda*. —— *Young Rake*, J. *Bafcow* from *Antigoa*, *Snow Vernon*, W. *Leacraft*. from *St. Chriftophers*, *Dove*, J. *Morgan*, from *Jamaica*, Brig. *Alexander*, J. *Leake*. *Belinder Keziah* C. *Gayton*, from *London*, *Snow James*, E. *May*. from *Swanzy*.

Outward Entries.
Sloop *Seanymph*, J. *Wickham*, for *S. Carolina*, Brig. *Aneram*, W. *Boyd*, junr. for *St. Chriftophers*, Ship *Seanymph*, O. *Guere*, for *Antigoa*, Sloop *Endeavour*, T. *Waterman*, for *Jamaica*, Ship *Nathaniel*, J. *Hayman*, for *Ireland*.

Cleared for Departure.
Sloop *Nightingale*, T. *Barnes*, junr. to *S. Carolina*, Brig. *Margaret*, J. *Walker*, to *Antigoa*, Sloop *Greenwich*. J. *Bufh*, —— *Royal Ranger*, R. *Mathelin*, to *Jamaica*. —— *Anne*, J. *Machet*, to *Coracoa*, Brig. *Induftry*, J. *Pearfe* to *Amfterdam*.

New-York, Printed by *John Peter Zenger*, where Advertifements are taken in.

cally ruled New York. A word from her meant life or death; only in an atmosphere of terror where logic surrendered to panic could such a situation have ocurred. The climate was right, and Mary Burton had the shrewdness to sense this; she seized her chance to gain glory.

SEVEN

The turning point of Mary Burton's life came on Monday, April 17. On that day, she was scheduled to appear before the grand jury which convened at City Hall with Judge Horsmanden presiding. Mary was to testify against Peggy Kerry and the Hughsons.

She rose before dawn that morning, although Horsmanden had excused her from all chores. She washed, combed and braided her lank hair, donned a clean dress, put on freshly polished shoes, and then sat primly in a straight-backed chair, staring at a spot on the wall, thinking hard, deciding how she would act and what she would say in court. The scope of the scheme she finally evolved almost overwhelmed Mary. Its success hinged on whether or not the Judge and jury would believe her. She had nailed Hughson easily enough; the cache of stolen goods supplied all the proof necessary. To put across what she had in mind, without tangible evidence, was going to be risky and difficult. If she failed, the punishment would be harsh—twenty lashes on the bared back. Perhaps she ought to stick to the facts: Hughson was a fence; the others his aides.

But the lure proved too tempting; a hundred pounds represented a fortune to her. It was worth any hazard to get such wealth. She did not intend to lose that money. A hundred pounds. To her mind, it was a king's ransom!

Mary rose and rehearsed her part. Standing in front of the mirror, she practiced looking shy, frightened, and bewildered, but always sincere and open; a poor, homeless waif who had come upon a terrible secret and had to unburden herself of it for the good of the community.

At last she was satisfied; her voice quavered properly with the exact tinge of fear, her face bore an expression of artless simplicity. There was no falseness, no guile in her frank eyes.

Smiling faintly, Mary sat down to rest. She knew the stern, powerful men would believe her because they were frightened. Despite their wealth and position, the Horsmandens, De Lanceys, and other prominent aristocrats were caught up in fear. Mary recognized this with her instinctive canniness.

An atmosphere of dread crept through the Horsmanden house. The impact of recent events had staggered the Judge. His world seemed about to crumble. All at once, he feared that the slaves would want more than scraps, ragged clothes, a lifetime of endless toil, and an unmarked grave in a swamp cemetery. They wanted freedom.

He was no cruel slaveowner; his bondsmen were seldom ill-treated. Usually the Judge trusted them fully. But since the fires and robberies, he watched his slaves carefully. Even Cordelia, the housekeeper, was not allowed to

73

keep the key ring that had been her mark of authority. She performed her duties sullenly, insulted that the master had demonstrated such a lack of faith in her loyalty.

In a rare outburst of temper, the Judge had slapped his coachman, Cato, and threatened him with a whipping for "insubordination," a charge without basis, stemming from the Judge's unnerved condition. Gentle, even-tempered Mrs. Horsmanden, driven by anxieties, lost her aplomb and berated the cook, Joanna, over some minor mistake. She even chastised the kitchen boys until they burst into tears. Joanna did her work in baleful silence, while the boys went around like small shadows.

Similar tensions had cropped up in every slaveowning household and shop. The formerly good relations between master and bondsman were blocked by a wall of distrust; in most cases the situation was becoming unbearable and an explosion seemed imminent.

"This unhappy community desires nothing more ardently than release from fear. If only we could root out the troublemakers and place them on the gibbet . . . ," a New Yorker lamented in a letter. His words reflected the prevailing opinion. Wealthy citizens and the authorities wanted a quick remedy for the city's ills. The method of finding it and the serious damage such a cure might cause the ailing city were not taken into consideration. New Yorkers did not care about consequences; they wanted a way out and would follow anyone who blazed a trail, no matter where it might lead.

On that Monday in April, Mary Burton became the city's guide. It was inconceivable that such a drab and ignorant individual could capture the minds of so many people. Actually, neither the Judge, the Attorney General, the jurors, or the onlookers regarded her as an instrument of salvation when she rose to face the grand jury as a witness in the case of the Crown vs. John Hughson *et al.* No one even paid much attention to her testimony as Attorney General Bradley asked her perfunctory questions about the Hogg robbery and the subsequent finding of the loot. The jury listened apathetically; Judge Horsmanden stifled a yawn; the spectators shifted in their seats.

Even the defendants seemed bored. Sara Hughson dozed, her mouth hanging open; Peggy Kerry flirted with a duty constable; John Hughson, the stubble dark on his chin and jowls, glared murderously at the witness; Mrs. Hughson kept wiping her streaming eyes, with a soiled handkerchief.

Mary shifted uneasily on her perch in the witness box. She gripped the railing hard, answering Bradley's queries in a low, uncertain voice that barely carried to the jurors. At the prosecution's prodding, she described how Hughson had hidden the stolen goods. She hesitated, fidgeted, and several times blanched when her eyes happened to light on Hughson. At last, her testimony was concluded.

A stir rippled through the courtroom as Bradley turned to Hughson's lawyer, Thomas Cowan, a shabbily dressed man of fifty, who badly needed clean linen and a shave. He had a drunkard's bulbous, red-veined nose, and his reputation was as disreputable as his appearance.

"Your witness, Mr. Cowan," Bradley said.

Cowan arose clumsily from his chair. He hicupped loudly, and everyone laughed. Obviously, he had been drinking. "No questions," the lawyer mumbled, and dropped heavily back into his seat.

"Damn it, what're you doin'?" Hughson whispered fiercely.

"It won't do any good, John," Cowan said. "They've got you cold. You're a gone goose!"

Horsmanden peered down from the bench with a disgusted expression. "Mr. Cowan, you are a disgrace to the legal profession," he said icily. Then, nodding at Mary, he smiled. "You are finished, child. You may step down, with the thanks of the Court."

Mary did not move. She clung to the railing with all her strength. Her heart thumped furiously. This was the time. She had to do it now or the chance would be lost. Quite unexpectedly, she was really frightened. There was no need for acting. Gasping for breath, she rallied her flagging courage. "No, Your Lordship. Not yet. I ain't done. There's more. Something I must tell—"

"Yes?" the Judge said, raising his eyebrows. She was delaying his court, and this displeased him. "Come on, speak up, girl!"

She felt cold sweat break out all over her body; her stomach churned and a noose seemed to be tightening around her throat. For an instant, she swayed dizzily. As though from a great distance, she heard the Judge saying, "Stop wasting our time. Speak or leave the witness box!"

Trembling violently, Mary forced herself to look up at the Judge. "Your Lordship—I—I'm scared—they'll kill me—I'm that scared . . . it's about the fires, Your Lordship!"

"The fires! You mean—? Good heavens, girl! What can you know of them?"

Every person in the courtroom was electrified. The spectators leaned forward expectantly. Indifferent jurors now sat bolt upright. Bailiffs, attendants, even Hughson, his wife, and the drink-befuddled Cowan looked attentive. Only Sara Hughson still slumped, her head lolling until her father jabbed her with his elbow. Startled, she snapped awake, blinked stupidly, and whined, "What? What do you want?"

Mary conquered her momentary panic. All at once, she regained complete control. Inwardly calm, she pretended to be nervous and frightened. Licking her lips, she said in a strained voice, "I—I can tell Your Lordship who gave the orders to set the fires . . ."

"Name him!" Horsmanden cried in an unjudicial tone.

"Me life won't be worth a farthing, sir. Please Your Lordship, I daren't say—"

"Mary, you must tell us. I order you to reveal any and all information. I promise you shall have protection. And,

77

should the black-hearted devil be caught and convicted, you will be well rewarded. Now, speak out," Horsmanden said.

"Aye, sir. But he is here in this courtroom. He'll kill me!" she quavered.

"Bailiffs! See that no one leaves this chamber. Some of you stand by the witness. I'll hold you responsible if harm befalls her," Horsmanden snapped.

Two bailiffs flanked the witness box. Another placed himself in front of it. A husky court attendant stood to block the door. The silence in the courtroom was broken only by a cough, a rustle, a whisper. Aware that everybody's attention was centered upon her, Mary prepared for the great moment. Pointing at John Hughson, she cried, "It's him! He's the man."

The tavern keeper let out a bellow of surprise and rage. "No! It's a lie! She's lying! I'll kill her!"

He charged forward and the bailiffs grabbed him. Mary screamed and collapsed in the witness box. With closed eyes she heard the uproar—curses, grunts, blows, shouts. A bench crashed over. The Judge was pounding with his gavel and shouting, "Clear the court! Clear the court!"

All the while the girl lay sprawled on the polished oaken boards. At last the furor subsided. A voice said, "Bring her into the Judge's chambers."

Mary went limp as she was lifted. She let her head wobble loosely from side to side in a well-simulated faint. Tempted to peek, she did not dare raise her eyelids as two men carried her across a threshold and placed her on a couch.

"Get some brandy. Hurry," a man said.

Someone raised Mary's head and held a brandy glass to her lips. She let the liquor dribble down her throat. She gagged, spluttered, and coughed while pretending to "revive." She moaned a few times, mumbled, "No . . . don't . . . kill . . . me" and then opened her eyes to see Judge Horsmanden bending over her. Behind him stood Attorney General Bradley and some other men she did not know. Several bailiffs were in the oak-panelled room.

"Oh, Judge Horsmanden. Your Lordship, I—Where's Hughson?" she cried in alarm.

"Don't mind him, child. That villain's under lock and key. He can't hurt you," the Judge assured her.

Mary sat up. "But there are others still at large. Sure as the sun'll rise tomorrow, they'll kill me. Oh, I'm a goner." She began crying, rocking back and forth. "A goner. They'll get me . . ."

Looking distressed, the Judge patted her shoulder. "Now, now, Mary. Pull yourself together. You mustn't carry on this way. I'll see that you're well protected."

"Ah, yes, Your Lordship. I'm sorry, sir. But I'm that upset." With a mighty effort, she stopped crying. Still sniffling, she smiled bravely at the Judge. "I'll be all right, Your Lordship."

Attorney General Bradley stepped forward. "You're a brave lass, Mary. If you feel up to it, I'd like a few words

79

with you. Those were serious charges you made against Hughson. Can you back them up?"

"Ah, yes, sir. That I can."

"Then, if you're up to it, please tell us all you can about this business," Bradley said.

Mary began unfolding a rambling story. According to her, Hughson, abetted by his wife, daughter, and Peggy Kerry, was the mastermind of a conspiracy to be carried out by Negroes and white bondsmen. Their purpose was to burn the city, then to massacre the slaveowners and their families. After the slaughter, Hughson would be proclaimed king, and the slave, Cuffee, appointed governor. Any white women who survived the holocaust would be turned over to the slaves taking part in the uprising.

After delivering this tidbit, Mary claimed she had accidentally discovered the plot one evening at the White Rose Tavern. She was in the cellar, busy with her chores, when Hughson, accompanied by his family and Peggy, with four Negroes—Prince, Caesar, Cuffee, and Quack—came down the stairs. She wanted to make her presence known, but when Hughson began discussing details of the plot, she was afraid to move and had remained hidden in the shadows, scarcely breathing.

"They'd have murdered me on the spot, had they found me," she said.

The most awful moment for her had been when she witnessed a "blood" oath, administered by Hughson. Each of the conspirators swore never to reveal the plot and sealed that pledge by drinking from a wine cup that contained human blood, according to Hughson.

The oath was effective, Mary emphasised. Had not Prince and Caesar gone to their deaths without betraying the conspiracy? She had realized at once that the plotters were dangerous, and decided, if possible, to spike their plans. Hoping the conspiracy would fall apart without leadership, she had denounced Hughson as a fence, but even this failed to stop the plotters.

It had been decided at the White Rose Tavern that Quack was to set ablaze the Governor's House, while Cuffee put the warehouse in the Fly Mart to the torch. The fires that followed were set by slaves Mary did not know; she believed that the Spanish Negroes were involved in the plot, men such as Lacey's Juan, De Lancey's Antonio, Mesnard's Antonio, Becker's Pablo, and McMullen's Augustine—all presently in jail on suspicion of arson. Mary was aware that she ran no risk in naming them. She also implied that numerous white bondsmen and indentured servants might well be implicated in the conspiracy.

This complicated story was recited with much stammering and floundering. Mary had to do a lot of improvising and, at first, feared she may have overplayed her hand. To weave a tale of such scope and make it convincing would have challenged a much sharper mind than Mary's. She had started the operation in order to collect the one hundred pounds reward money—but as she stumbled and fumbled, that prize seemed far away indeed. At any moment she expected Bradley or Horsmanden to call her bluff. She need not have worried. Each time she faltered,

81

either the Judge or the Attorney General guided her cleverly back onto the path by asking leading questions. Horsmanden and all the other distinguished gentlemen present chose to take Mary's unsupported tale at face value. They all had been badly shaken during recent weeks and in a state close to panic. Men not already corroded by such fear probably would have seen through Mary's crude lies. But these apprehensive New Yorkers accepted the girl's fantasies as truth. They believed her because she was giving them flesh-and-blood enemies—Negro slaves, white bondsmen, Spaniards, the Hughsons, Peggy Kerry—instead of formless, faceless shadows. These foes could be dealt with on the gallows or at the stake. They could be tortured, maimed, and killed.

When the grand jury reconvened two days later at Attorney General Bradley's request, the story of the conspiracy had been deeply implanted in the public's mind. Few doubted such a plot existed; they questioned only its size. Bradley, for one, appeared convinced that a large number of slaves and others were involved. The chunky, rosy-cheeked lawyer, who seemed more like a genial grocer than a ruthless prosecutor, openly stated: "The Burton girl has provided us with a weapon that shall forever eliminate the dangers of an uprising by bondsmen whether Black or white. . . ." He told a group of leading citizens: "I shall not rest until the last conspirator pays with his life. . . . I intend to keep the public executioner busy in the weeks to come. No plotter can expect mercy from me."

Despite such public utterances, Bradley doubted that

Mary had told the truth. Her story smacked too much of the old yarns about the 1712 insurrection. He also thought that the Hughsons and the Kerry woman seemed unlikely organizers of such a conspiracy. As a lawyer, Bradley had noted many flaws and discrepancies in Mary Burton's account; he felt she wanted to collect the one hundred pounds and had fabricated the slave plot out of her imagination. At another time, Bradley would have shown up the girl as a liar and troublemaker.

However, he was a product of his day and his social class. A slaveowner himself, he feared a Negro uprising and would use any means to suppress one. The testimony of this alleged eyewitness to a conspiratorial meeting, coupled with the fears raised by the fires, were reasons enough for Bradley to suppress his personal feelings, compromise his integrity, and go ahead with the prosecution of the so-called plotters.

Prior to Mary's appearance before the grand jury, Bradley spent several hours ironing out the numerous flaws in her tangled yarn to make it sound more plausible. The Attorney General promised the girl an extra one hundred pounds payable when the conspirators had been rounded up and sentenced; she had only to change her story a bit here and there so the jurors could follow it with greater ease.

Mary snatched at the offer.

EIGHT

If Bradley had reservations about Mary, he revealed none of them during the grand-jury session. That panel met on Monday, April 17, to hear Mary Burton testify. The jurors listened raptly as she described the menacing situation in the city. Bradley remained in the background, coming forward only to help her fill in gaps by asking pointed questions. He was probably worried that the jurors would see through the thin material of Mary's narrative. Bradley might have spared himself this concern. The grand jury swallowed the girl's farfetched story and returned conspiracy indictments against all those she had named and "persons unknown." The verdict was reached within ten minutes, and the jurors did not even bother to leave the box for deliberation.

After complimenting the jury on its "intelligent decision," Judge Horsmanden remanded Quack and Cuffee to trial on May 1. The slaves would be only the first in a parade of defendants to face New York justice in the weeks ahead.

Ordinarily, slaves were denied the right of trial by jury, but in this case, Bradley requested that this prohibition be waived. "I want the defendants to enjoy every benefit of Anglo-Saxon law," he said. "This matter is too serious for usual procedures. Let a jury decide the outcome of the trial. I want no word of complaint that the accused were not fairly adjudged. . . ."

Bradley, of course, failed to add that the chances of a

jury acquitting the slaves were overwhelmingly small. Nor did he make clear precisely how an unbiased, open-minded jury could be found in New York City at that time. Popular sentiment was feverishly high against everyone concerned in the conspiracy; rumor, gossip, and agitators had blown Mary Burton's fiction into unquestioned fact. The public's animosity toward the accused had caused several near riots when unruly mobs marched on the prison to lynch them. Only the presence of troops stopped the crowds. It was unlikely that anyone could be "fairly adjudged" in such an atmosphere. A change of venue was in order, but no attorney in New York would defend or advise the defendants, a circumstance which further hampered their chances in court.

Bradley's gesture in seeking a jury trial did not jeopardize the prosecution. He knew that the jurors had to be selected from a list of white property holders, many of whom also owned slaves. Such men were not likely to spare rebellious slaves or those who led them. The Attorney General was confident of winning a guilty verdict; however, he did not want the men who owned Quack and Cuffee or any other slave to blame either Judge Horsmanden or himself for the verdict and its mandatory death penalty. The sentences would be the collective responsibility of the jurors. The Judge and he were bound to emerge from the trial as staunch defenders of the social order, in no way subject to any reproach from the disgruntled masters who had lost their slaves through judicial action.

The Attorney General had one small problem to overcome before the trial. At least two prosecution witnesses were needed under New York law in capital cases, as otherwise there could be no conviction. Since Bradley's whole case depended upon Mary Burton, he needed someone to corroborate her testimony. He soon found a man willing to commit perjury in return for a favor from the prosecutor. Bradley's confederate was a thief named Arthur Price, currently serving a three-year term in prison. For the promise of a parole, Price agreed to testify that Quack and Cuffee had revealed their part in the conspiracy to him in jail. Bradley arranged to have Price transferred to a cell adjoining that occupied by the slaves; the prosecutor's spy tried to make friends with the two Negroes, but Cuffee sensed that he was an informer and warned Quack to ignore the white man.

When Price reported this turn, Bradley was undisturbed. He would put the man on the stand anyway, after coaching him on what testimony to give. Only the fact that the defendants had no lawyer enabled Bradley to use such tactics. He was overstepping his bounds by calling on a convicted felon to testify. In New York, at that time, a criminal under prison sentence had no standing in court and should not have been allowed to serve as a witness. However, it was the burden of the defense to raise an objection; owing to the lawyer boycott, Quack and Cuffee were forced to defend themselves. Since they were totally ignorant of the law, Price was able to deliver his damaging falsehoods against them.

The thief blandly stated that the slaves had confessed their guilt to him and exposed the entire conspiracy in a flood of confidences. His version jibed perfectly with that given by Mary Burton. The trial, which was a mockery, had an inevitable and predictable outcome. It was bad enough that Bradley resorted to shabby tactics, but it was even worse that Quack and Cuffee had to act as their own counsel. Both men were illiterate and could barely comprehend what was going on. Their only defense was to insist that both Mary Burton and Arthur Price were lying. The jurors were not impressed, and quickly returned a guilty verdict. Judge Horsmanden sentenced them to be burned at the stake on May 30; the execution was held off until then because the authorities hoped the condemned men now would talk freely about the conspiracy.

Governor Clarke was lavish in his praise of Bradley and cited him for his efficiency and high purpose in "safeguarding and maintaining the peace of the colony." The prosecutor was mentioned in the Governor's report to London and recommended for a decoration.

In the same dispatch, Governor Clarke described Judge Horsmanden as an "indefatigable defender of the Crown . . . a model of judicial deportment and a jurist of the highest calibre. . . ." He, too, was put in for a royal award.

Although both prosecutor and Judge were fully aware that the trial had been rigged and that the existence of a conspiracy was dubious, both devoted themselves energetically to "discover, expose and punish the conspirators. . . ." The figments of Mary Burton's imagination had become vividly real.

The Attorney General put pressure upon the doomed slaves, urging them to make full confessions, even dangling before them a vague hope of clemency if they admitted their guilt and revealed their co-conspirators. Since Quack and Cuffee had nothing to confess, both steadfastly maintained complete innocence. Realizing he could squeeze nothing more from the pair, Bradley gave up and ordered that the executions be held on schedule.

Almost everyone in New York, Negro and white, turned out to watch the slaves burn. Stakes were erected on The Collect Island, each piled high with faggots, ready for the torch. The day of the execution, Tuesday, May 30, was an unofficial holiday. The weather was bright and pleasant. Many spectators, seeking a vantage spot, came early, bringing along baskets of food. The occasion was turned into a family outing; children romped in the grass, shouting and laughing.

At noon, a tremendous yell went up from the audience as a boat bearing the chained and manacled prisoners was rowed out to the island. Another boat carried city officials and the public executioner, his face covered with a black, conical hood. The terrified prisoners, screaming for mercy, were dragged to the stakes. Their cries carried across the water to the onlookers, who chanted "Burn 'em! Burn 'em!"

In a last desperate attempt to save themselves, both men babbled a confession of guilt. Cuffee, who was more rational, made a clear statement: Hughson had contrived the plot and given the orders to start the fires. Neither Quack nor he ever had met any other conspirators except Prince and Caesar. Both slaves agreed that Mrs. Hughson, her daughter, and Peggy Kerry had full knowledge of the plot's details. In fact, it was Sara who had marked on a city map the places to be burned.

Lyman Miles, the Undersheriff of New York City, who had charge of the execution, ordered the doomed men returned to jail. Constables started leading them back to the boat. However, when the people on shore realized what was taking place, a roar of protest arose. They had come to see Quack and Cuffee consigned to the flames and were not going to be cheated out of that spectacle. Groups of young whites ran down to the water's edge and began hurling rocks at Miles and his constables. Frustrated anger caused fist fights in the crowd. Mothers, with bawling children, ran away screaming. Rocks, bottles, and debris sailed through the air. A dozen boats carrying cursing roughs sped toward the island.

Undersheriff Miles, no martyr to duty, saw that a riot was imminent, reversed his decision, and told the executioner to proceed. This mollified the mob, which settled down again in relative calm. The slaves were lashed to the stakes and the piled-up faggots set alight. The flames roared high within seconds. . . .

P. S. I am ready to conduct any *Welshman*, or others, to the Country.

I shall next make some Remarks on the above Letter.

It appears by this Narrative, that the Author, Mr. *Morgan Jones*, was probably unacquainted with the History of his own Country. He was surpriz'd (ane well he might) to hear the *Doeg Indians* talk the *British* Language; and concludes (and indeed very justly) that they must be descended from the Old *Britons*; but *when* and *how*, our Author seems to be at a Loss. But the *Welsh* History (first wrote by *Caradoc*, Abbot of *Llancarvan*, and since publish'd by Dr. *Powel* sets the whole Matter in a clear Light, and unravels the Mystery. For it informs us, that in the Year 1170, *Madoc ap Owen Gwyneth* (to avoid the Calamities and Distractions of a civil War at Home) took a Resolution to go in Quest of some remote Country to live in Peace. And so having directed his Course due West, he landed in some Place of that vast Continent now called *America*. There, being charmed with the Fertility of the Soil (after having built some slight Fortifications for the Security of his People) he returns home to *North-Wales*, leaving 120 Men behind. There reciting his successful Voyage, and describing the fruitful and pleasant Land he found out, he prevail'd with many of his Country People, Men and Women, to return with him to enjoy that Tranquility in a remote Country, which they could not in their own. The brave Adventurers put out to Sea in Ten Barges, laden with all manner of Necessaries, and by GOD's Providence landed safely in the same Harbour they arriv'd at before: It is very probable it was about *Mexico*, since there Prince *Madoc* was bury'd; as his Epitaph since found there, does make evident beyond all Contradiction.

> *Madoc wyf mwydic ei wedd*
> *Jawn genau Owen Gwynedd;*
> *Ni fynnwn dir, fy awydd oedd*
> *Na da mawr ondy Moroedd.*

It is indeed the common Opinion, that in the Course of a few Generations, *Madoc* and his Men incorporated with the Natives, and made one People with them; whence proceed the various *British* Words that the *Europeans* found among the *Mexico Indians*; such as, *Pengwyn, Groeso, Gwenddwr, Bara, Tad, Mam, Buwch, Clugiar, Llywynog, Coch y dwr*, with many more recited in Sir *Thomas Herbert's Travels*, p. 222. But by this Narrative it is evident, that they keep as yet a distinct People, at least in the Year 1660, when our Author was amongst them. For Mr. *Jones* says, he not only convers'd with them about the ordinary Affairs of Life, but *preached to them three Times a Week in the British Language*; and that they usually consulted him when any Thing appeared difficult in the same Language; which evidently demonstrates, that they still preserve their Original Language, and are still a Colony or People unmixed.

Now if a premier Discovery confers a Right (as it seems it is a Maxim in Politicks) then the Crown of *England* has an indisputable Right to the Sovereignty of these Countries in *America*; for the *Spania ds* had no Footing there 'til the Year 1492, 322 Years since the first Discovery by Prince *Madoc*. Some Statesmen indeed would fain have persuaded Queen *Elizabeth* to insist on this Title (as is mentioned by Dr. *Heylin*, p. 1000. Ed. 3. of his Geography.) But they had only an obscure Tradition *then*, that was thought would not bear Proof: But this Narrative sets off the whole Matter beyond Dispute; wherein our Author writes with such Simplicity and unaffected Style, and without any studied Eloquence, as 'tis plain he had nothing in View, but to relate the naked Truth. And since this is a Matter of Fact so well attested, backed with such Variety of Incidents, let not the proud *Dons* any more assume the Glory of this noble Discovery; but let our most puissant Monarch of *Great Britain* claim his most just Rights.

—*BRITONS STRIKE HOME!*
> *Theophilus Evans*, Vicar of
> St. *David's*, in *Brecon*.

NEW-YORK.

In a former Paper, we gave an Account that two Negroes were burnt here, who at the Stake, Confessed they were guilty of the Crimes, for which they suffered and discovered the Plot, and Conspiracy formed here and in Part carried into Execution, since which we have learned, that this most horrible and wicked Conspiracy, has been a long time in agitation, and almost general among the Negroes, *John Huson*, (executed last Week, with his Wife and *Margaret Kerry*,) was a Contriver and grand Promoter er of this detestable Scene of Villany, which was Calculated, not only to ruin & destroy this City, but the whole Province, and it appears that to Effect this their Defign, was firft to burn the Fort, and if Opportunity favoured to feize and Carry away the Arms in Store there, then to burn the whole Town, and kill and Murder all the Male Inhabitants thereof (the Females they intending to referve for their own ufe) and this to be Effected by feizing their Mafter's Arms and a general rifing It appears alfo as we are informed that thefe Defigns were not only carried on in this City but had alfo fpread into the Country.

And that the *Spanifh* Negroes (of which there are many in this Place) were deeply concerned and active in the Bufinefs; and whatever Encouragement or Affurances they might recieve from abroad, or hellifh Incendiaries at home, they were perfwaded that an attempt on this Province would be made by the *Spaniards* and *French* for whom they agreed to wait fome Time; And if it fhould happen that fuch an Attempt fhould be made, and our Enemies invade us; they were to rife and join with them. *Hufon* having bought and procured Arms, Ammunition and Powder for that purpofe; and if fuch an Invafion fhould not happen, They were then to carry their diabollickal Scheme into Execution themfelves. And fo far had they gone that the Particular Places to be firft burnt where laid out, their Captains and other Officers appointed, and their Places of general Rendevous fixed, and the Number of Negroes concern'd is almoft incredible, and their Barbarous Defigns ftill more fo, efpecially when it is Confidered that white People were privy to and fomenters of fo unparalel'd a Villany, which was by keeping their invention fo Privately laid, and the concerned fo artfully bound by the moft horrid and Execrable Oaths, that in all probability it would have remained a Secret till they had done much more Mifchief, but by the Mercy of God and through the Indefatigable pains and Vigilance of the Magiftracy, and the prefent worthy Grand Jury, their Deeds of Darknefs are now we hope almoft (if not quite) brought to a full Light.

Since our laft 15 Negroes have been capitally convicted whereof 7 have been burnt 1 reprieved, and 2 have been pardoned on their Confeffions, and five are to receive Sentence this Day; *Hufon*, his Wife and *Margaret Kerry*, have been hanged, and *Sarah* the Daughter of *Hufon* reprieved, 5 *Spanifh* Negroes have been alfo arraigned and are this Day to be tryed, and many more are now in Goal. As foon as we can obtain a full Account of this Plot and Leave from the Magiftrates we fhall publifh the fame.

ADVERTISEMENTS.

TO

NINE

Excitement was at a peak in New York after the executions of Quack and Cuffee. Everyone had the conspiracy on his mind. It overshadowed every aspect of city life. Anxious fathers shepherded their children to school; men went about their daily business with pistols tucked in waistbands. Slaves did their chores eying one another furtively, trying to guess if this one or that one were involved in the plot.

Seldom had any city been so torn by distrust and suspicion. Slaves who had served faithfully for years were regarded as possible traitors. Master artisans watched indentured apprentices closely. The white bondsmen and servants were considered as potentially dangerous as the Negroes.

Some men flourished in this atmosphere of hatred and apprehension. Horsmanden and Bradley rose to greater importance than ever before. Hailed as the protectors of the city, the two men easily assumed their roles as bulwarks of justice. A peculiar metamorphosis took place in them; each thought of himself as a champion against the peril that threatened to wipe out their social system.

"Any doubts or qualms I might have had in the recent past are now dispelled," Bradley wrote. "There is no longer a question that the conspiracy is real. . . . My deeds today shall decide the fate of future generations. . . . I will not fail them!"

In a similar vein, Horsmanden noted, "I must tear the word mercy from my lexicon until this evil is ended. . . .

I shall liquidate every conspirator, Black or white, until we are rid of this blight upon our once tranquil lives. . . . It is my God-given duty to serve as the shield of Justice. . . .

Little dissent or disapproval hampered Horsmanden and Bradley; masters of the executed slaves grumbled, but reluctantly agreed that what had been done was necessary. That Mary Burton, the dubious source of the conspiracy charges, was never seriously challenged did not seem strange at the time. The Salem Witch Trials had been sparked by evidence no stronger than that offered by Mary Burton.

Mary prospered more than anyone from the situation she had generated. Had she not touched off the conspiracy panic, the drab girl would have passed her life in drudgery. Instead, she basked in glory and praise, relishing her newly won fame and importance. Judge Horsmanden no longer regarded her as an indentured servant. He had, in fact, cancelled Mary's indenture and declared her free of any obligations to it.

She was moved to a room in the main wing of the house and outfitted with fine new clothes. The Judge and his wife considered her their ward; Mrs. Horsmanden taught her some table manners so she could dine with the family, waited on by her former co-workers of the kitchen. Although the girl did not completely shed her former crudities, she at least gave a more presentable appearance. She flounced haughtily, ordering the servants about. They resented and feared her, well aware that Mary had brought about the deaths of four men. A slovenly person, she left her room in an untidy condition, with clothes strewn about. One morning, Cordelia chided her for being so sloppy.

"Don't sass me!" Mary snapped. "You do your work or I'll make you mighty sorry."

Cordelia bristled. "Young woman, not even the master and the mistress give me such talk. I'll not have it from a guttersnipe!"

"Guttersnipe, eh?" Mary shouted. "You'll eat that word! Now get out! Get out!"

The housekeeper left the room, slamming the door hard. Mary stood glowering after her. She did not yet feel secure enough to lodge a complaint about Cordelia with the Judge. She'd have to wait and settle things with the housekeeper another day. Yes, and with Joanna, too. Mary hadn't forgotten how the cook once had threatened her with a whipping. Very well. They'd get what was coming to them. An eye for an eye. She could wait, just as she had done with Cordelia.

Once, Mary remembered a sermon she had heard in the orphanage, a long time ago. She could only recall a single phrase of what had been said: ". . . the mills of God grind slowly. . . ." Yes. Mary Burton ground slowly and her enemies were crushed. Time was the secret. Time to wait and then to pounce like a cat on an unwary bird. A little patience. A little more time.

Suddenly, a disturbing thought crossed her mind. The Kerry woman and the Hughsons would be tried in a few days. Once she finished her testimony, Horsmanden surely wouldn't keep her in his house. She'd go back to—what? Her former grubby existence? No. It wouldn't be quite the same. She'd collect the two hundred pounds reward, and that wasn't a trifle. Ah, but now she knew money wasn't the whole story. There was more; she'd had a taste of being somebody, of feeling power.

That was what she couldn't give up. Two hundred pounds wouldn't last forever. When it was gone—what then? Back to a scullery somewhere, scrubbing pots, washing floors, eating slops, wearing rags?

Not Mary Burton. That was all behind her. There was a way to keep hanging on. She had mastered the technique of the big lie, of making people believe her; all she had to do was play on their fears.

The gentry would listen to anything she told them, and she meant to hold their interest for a long time to come. All that remained was to invent a suitable story for use after the Hughsons and Kerry danced on air. She never doubted for a second that they would be sentenced to the gallows.

Her problem was to be convincing. She sat down on the bed and thought hard. After a while, she had a plan of action. . . .

TEN

The second conspiracy case, the Crown vs. John Hughson *et al,* went to court on Monday, June 11, a day of stifling heat and humidity. Despite the torrid temperature, the courtroom was packed with rapt spectators. A jury was soon chosen. The only difference between this trial and the first one was that the defendants had a lawyer, Thomas Cowan, the same rum-pot attorney who had represented Hughson before the grand jury. He had been the only attorney willing to accept the assignment. Judge Horsmanden had insisted that the accused have counsel only because they were white. It would have been unseemly to put them in the same category as slaves.

As in the previous trial, Bradley relied upon only two witnesses—Mary Burton and Arthur Price. The former told her by now familiar tale, while Price added some trimmings. According to him, Sara, Peggy Kerry, and Mrs. Hughson had admitted their guilt to him in prison.

This sort of testimony would have been torn to shreds by a capable defense attorney. Cowan was not even competent. But Cowan only asked a few routine questions in cross-examination, put the badly rattled Hughson on the stand, and followed him with the weeping Mrs. Hughson, hysterical Sara, and Peggy Kerry, who lost her composure and shrilled abusively at Mary, Price, the Judge, the prosecutor, and the jurors. Her conduct did not help the defendants.

Bradley never bothered to question the accused. Instead, he rested his case and delivered a dramatic speech to the jury in summation, calling upon them to: ". . . defend your homes, your families and your honor. . . . Shall such execrable villains miss their deserved punishment and escape the justice of the law? The decision, gentlemen of the jury, rests with you!"

Cowan, the defense attorney, made a fumbling address to the jury that did his clients no good. The verdict was swift. "Guilty as charged." The sentence, passed by Horsmanden, surprised no one: "The defendants shall be taken hence, to the place of execution and there shall be hanged by the neck until dead, dead, dead!"

Bradley then called upon the Judge to grant Sara Hughson a temporary reprieve in the hope that she would co-operate with the authorities in their efforts to ". . . uncover additional miscreants involved in this dastardly plot. . . ."

The Judge readily acceded to the prosecution request, and the defendants were led away. Peggy Kerry and the Hughsons were hanged two days later, while Sara howled inconsolably in her cell. Her ordeal was far from over. Bradley or one of his assistants came daily to ply her with questions. They pressed the bereft girl for more details of the plot, reminding her constantly that the hangman awaited. Of course, Sara had nothing to tell them. On June 19, about a week after her parents' execution, she was again scheduled to be hanged, but Governor Clarke granted another stay because Bradley still felt that Sara might yet prove useful.

The Attorney General was reluctant to see the conspiracy trials come to an end. He saw them as a means to rise higher in the colonial administration; Bradley had his eye on the governorship, an ambition that could be realized if he gained even greater repute as the man who had smashed the slave conspiracy. The pot was kept boiling for him by two or three unrelated incidents.

First, Georgia's Governor Oglethorpe sent another letter to Clarke repeating his warning that Spanish agents were at large in all the English colonies. Once again Oglethorpe cautioned that "disguised Catholic priests" prepared to commit acts of "sabotage and destruction" probably had filtered into New York. Their best henchmen, Oglethorpe declared, would well be "the slaves of Spanish extraction . . ."

A score or more of Spanish Negro slaves were then in jail, but there was nothing to link them with any plot, nor was there any indication that they were aiding enemy agents. Bradley had arrested them purely on suspicion. In her original charges, Mary Burton never had mentioned these men, so the prosecutor could not bring them to trial. He had no witnesses, not even perjured ones, to testify against the Spaniards. However, events mitigated in his behalf. The Spanish Negro, Juan de la Sylva, known as Lacey's Juan, broke out of jail on June 20. In making his escape, de la Sylva slugged a guard and stole his pistol.

The slave's act raised a furor. Soldiers, constables, slave catchers, and volunteers searched everywhere for him without success. Somehow a rumor was started that the fugitive was hiding with a priest who was posing as a fencing master. There were only four fencing masters in New York; three had been residents of the city for a long time and were well known. The fourth, John Ury, was a new-comer, having arrived only a few months earlier just before the outbreak of the fires.

A slim, mild-mannered man of thirty with sandy hair and blue eyes, Ury had such talent with rapier and saber that he quickly gained repute as a teacher of fencing. Many of the city's wealthy young bloods came to him for instruction. An accomplished linguist, he spoke fluent French, Italian, and Spanish; he also was well schooled in Latin and Greek. His background remained a secret, for he was closemouthed about his past. He admitted to having lived in London until forced to leave under mysterious circumstances.

It was whispered that he had slain a nobleman's son in a duel over a girl. Except for maintaining silence about his life in England, Ury was a garrulous person. He liked to discuss religious matters and used Latin freely in these theological disputes.

Unfortunately for him, most New Yorkers had peculiar ideas about the way to unmask a Roman Catholic priest. They suspected anyone who had a tendency to religious disputation and was fluent in Latin. These traits made Ury a prime suspect in the hunt for the "disguised Catholic priests" mentioned in Oglethorpe's letters. The fact that he was a fencing master also aroused suspicion. However, Bradley hesitated to arrest him. The man was popular and had many influential friends; the Attorney General needed stronger evidence before moving against Ury.

The third event set the stage for the final act in the so-called New York Slave Conspiracy. A few nights after the slave Juan's escape, Judge Horsmanden held a musicale at his home. A string quartet was playing for an audience made up of New York's high society. Suddenly, the genteel atmosphere was shattered by a terrible shriek outside the parlor window. Everyone rushed out to find Mary Burton running toward them across the broad lawn, screaming at the top of her voice. She clutched her right arm. Blood flowed from a gash between the fingers of her left hand.

While the wound was being dressed, the girl claimed that a man she knew to be the fugitive Spanish slave had stabbed her. Although the knife slash was superficial, it bled profusely. Mary told the white-faced listeners that she had gone for a stroll, and Juan de la Sylva had leaped out from behind some bushes, brandishing a knife.

"Traitor!" he hissed, lunging at her with the blade.

Luckily his thrust had only pierced her hand. The slave fled when she screamed. Searchers rushed out to look for the Spaniard but failed to find him. Mary told Horsmanden that she had feared an attack since exposing the plot. In fact, she said, there was more to that ugly story than she had revealed. On New Year's Eve, December 31, 1740, a big party had been held at Hughson's tavern with almost a hundred Negroes and whites present. As the whites looked on approvingly, each slave had sworn to burn his master's house and then vowed to "go out and kill all whites" except those at the party, their families and friends." According to Mary most of the Spanish Negroes had been there openly whetting their knives.

She had not previously described this occurrence in the hope that the authorities would deal with the Spaniards. Even after de la Sylva's escape, knowing her life was in danger, she had maintained silence. When asked why she had not spoken then, the girl replied, "I feared no one would believe me. There was no proof except my word."

"Child, that's good enough for us!" Horsmanden exclaimed. "You should not have waited so long, putting your life in jeopardy—"

"I wanted to cause no trouble, sir."

"Trouble, indeed! You're a fine, patriotic young lady," Horsmanden said. "This colony owes you a great debt for the heroic work you've done."

(Perhaps Horsmanden would have been less generous with his praise if he had known that Mary's knife wound was self-inflicted. She had slashed her hand, hidden the weapon, and made up the whole story. It is almost certain that at the time she claimed de la Sylva had attacked her, he was dead by his own hand in The Marsh. His body was discovered months later, with a note in his own tongue pinned to the moldering coat; the message said: "I prefer death with honor and at my own choice rather than to die like an animal before the eyes of cruel and vicious oppressors. . . .")

The next morning, closely guarded by two constables, Mary went before the grand jury, which had been summoned in an emergency session by Attorney General Bradley. The girl plunged, without hesitation, into a vivid account of Hughson's New Year's Eve party. She rattled off a list of those who had been there. By the end of the day's session, the prosecutor ordered the arrests of many Negroes, including Horsmanden's own slaves—Joanna, Cordelia, and Cato.

Shocked to learn that his favorites had participated in the plot, the Judge turned a deaf ear to their protestations of innocence and watched impassively as they were taken away. He was suffering no more than other slaveowners who had lost their property.

However, Mary's wholesale denunciations were far from over. She had heard that John Ury was under suspicion as a Catholic priest. She did not know Ury, but this did not faze her. Suddenly and conveniently, Mary remembered that a masked man had turned up at the party just after midnight. He had conducted a series of weird rituals in a foreign tongue which she presumed to be Latin. Although she had not seen his face, the girl asserted that she could recognize his voice. No one even bothered to question how it was possible for an uneducated servant to know whether or not Latin was spoken.

A warrant was issued for Ury on Mary's fragile testimony. But still she was not through. Even as constables were going out to make the arrests, Mary spewed more names, denouncing anyone she could recall from among the customers of the White Rose. She talked with a compulsion that bordered on madness. She named four soldiers of the garrison—William Kane, Edward Murphy, Brian Donovan, and Andrew Ryan—who happened to be Catholics. In a short time she had hurled accusations at about thirty whites—seamen, peddlers, mechanics, bondsmen, stevedores, and carters—who frequented the tavern.

It pleased Bradley that some Catholics were included among the new batch of suspects—this lent weight to the myth of a "papist-inspired" plot.

The colonies' sanctimonious officials pressed their prosecution with enthusiasm. John Ury was caught up in the crusade. Seized at his *salle d'armes,* the fencing master argued that no basis existed for his arrest. When Bradley accused him of "conducting papist ceremonies," Ury cried, "By my soul, I've never been a Catholic!"

His protests were futile and convinced no one.

ELEVEN

The authorities wasted no time. Only a few days after Mary's latest denunciations, a mass trial of twenty Spanish Negroes was held. There were no legal trappings to block the path of justice; the proceedings resembled a drumhead court-martial rather than a trial. A hand-picked jury heard the prosecution demand the death penalty for each defendant. No lawyer represented the accused. Nor were the charges or testimony translated into Spanish.

Bradley had one witness—the ubiquitous Mary Burton—who reiterated her version of the New Year's Eve party at the White Rose. The jury accepted her narrative without comment or reservation. Several of the masters of the Spaniards—all respectable members of the community —spoke up in court for their charges but could not sway the jurors. Within a half hour, a guilty verdict was returned.

Horsmanden sentenced twelve of the twenty defendants to the gallows, and the rest were ordered shipped to the West Indies, a terrible fate. Slaves rarely survived the hard labor, harsh treatment, climate, yellow fever, malaria, and other diseases rampant in the islands. The Judge's gesture was pointed up to show foreign observers that New York justice was not "vindictive," although being transported to the West Indies was tantamount to a drawn-out sentence of death.

The twelve Spaniards were hanged the day after sentence had been passed. This undue haste aroused bitter criticism of the authorities by the slaveowners. One man who lost three bondsmen bluntly stated: "I fear that the officials of this colony have lost their senses. It is a sorry day when presumedly rational men are swayed by the allegations of a kitchen wench."

Governor George Clarke was highly sensitive to such comment. He responded at once with a most unusual proclamation that was intended to "erase the menace now threatening our beloved province. . . ." Clarke declared

"I am empowered to offer His Majesty's most gracious pardon to any and every person, whether white, slave or others who had been or were concerned in the conspiracy . . . who shall, before July 1, 1741, voluntarily, freely and fully confess his, her or their confederates, accomplices or others concerned in said conspiracy. . . . All who comply will be fully pardoned . . ."

A hanging on the Commons, 1741.

THE

New-York Weekly JOURNAL.

Containing the freſheſt Advices, Foreign, and Domeſtick.

MUNDAY June 29th, 1741.

By the HONOURABLE.

George Clarke, Eſq; His Majeſty's Lieutenant Governour and Commander in Chief of the Province of *New-York*, and the Teritories thereon depending in *America.*

A PROCLAMATION.

WHEREAS a moſt Wicked and Dangerous Conſpiracy has been lately formed and ſet on foot in this City and Province, abetted, encouraged and carried on by ſeveral *White People*, in Conjunction with divers *Spaniſh Negroe*'s lately brought over from the *Weſt Indies*, and a great Number of the other *Negroes* within this City and Country, for burning and deſtroying of this whole Town and City, and for the Murdering the Inhabitants thereof, to the utter Ruin and Deſtruction of the whole Province. For which Diabolical Scheme and Conſpiracy a great Number of *Slaves* and others, have already been Convicted and Executed, and many others are now indicted and Impriſoned, in order for their Tryal for the ſaid Offences.

But to the End that Mercy may be ſhewn to ſuch as may merit and deſerve the ſame, I have thought it neceſſary, and I do hereby, by and with Advice of His Majeſty's Council, in His Majeſty's Name, Iſſue this Proclamation, hereby Offering and Promiſing His Majeſty's moſt Gracious Pardon to any and every Perſon or Perſons, whether White People, Free Negroes, Slaves, or others, who have been or are concerned in the ſaid Conſpiracy, who ſhall, on or before the firſt Day of *July* next, voluntarily, freely and fully diſcover and Conſeſſion make of his, her or their Confederates, Accomplices, or others concerned in the ſaid Conſpiracy, and his, her or their part or ſhare, actings and doings therein, ſo that the Perſons making ſuch diſcovery

and Confeſſion be not before Convicted, Arreigned or Indicted for the ſame.

Given under my Hand and Seal at New-York, *the Nineteenth Day of* June, *in the Fifteenth year of His Majeſty's Reign, Annoq; Domini,* 1741.

GEORGE CLARKE.

On the 12th *Inſtant a Petition was preſented to the Aſſembly ſetting forth.*

That a horrid Conſpiracy has been lately formed by ſome Wicked White People, in Confedracy with a great Number of Negro Slaves, to lay this City in Aſhes, and to Murder and deſtroy the Inhabitants thereof, which has been, in part, executed, by burning His Majeſty's Houſe, and other Publick buildings in the Fort, and by ſetting fire to ſundry other Houſes in this City, by which Conſpiracy great Terror and Diſtreſs, and very conſiderable Loſs and Damage has been brought upon the Inhabitants of this City. And that upon ſtrict Enquiry, the great Number of Publick Houſes in which Negroes have been entertained and encouraged to buy Rum and other ſtrong Liquors, has been a principal Inſtrument to their Diabolical Vilanies. And that the horrid Conſpiracy to burn this City and to Murder the People, was formed and agreed to by great Numbers of Negroes meeting together on divers Sundays, and was intended to be put in Execution on ſome Sunday Morning during the Time of Publick Service; as alſo fetching Tea-Water on Sundays, has been found to tend to the forming of the ſaid Conſpiracy, by giving Occaſion to great Numbers of them to meet in the ſame Place, that ſome further Proviſion by Law to prevent the like Evils for the future, will be of abſolute neceſſity for the Peace and Safety of this City, and worthy

of

Governor Clark's proclamation as reported in Zenger's *New York Weekly Journal,* June 29, 1741. The version of the proclamation in the text is taken from Horsmanden's papers.

It was stressed that no confession would be considered valid unless the person making it implicated someone else. "In this fashion," Clarke said, "we shall ferret out the guilty. . . ."

From the Governor's point of view, this edict had a very desirable effect. Within hours after its publication, most of the jailed Negroes and whites indicated that they wanted to talk. The accused became accusers. Men and women poured out names of "accomplices" and "fellow conspirators," whether or not those mentioned could have logically played any part in the plot. Before long it appeared as though most of the slaves and many whites in the city were involved. Judge Horsmanden noted in a letter: ". . . so many Negroes have begun to squeak that the jail is crowded to the bursting point. . . ."

The rush to confess turned into a unchecked panic. Insanity seemed to have overtaken the city. All sorts of wild and irrational tales were spilled. A Negro, Jack, cleared himself by naming six other slaves as plotters, among them his own brother. One man claimed to have known about the plot for more than three years. Bastian, a slave, told Bradley that the long-dead Hagar had given Hughson enough poison "to foul all the fish in the rivers."

As quickly as accused persons were released from prison after confessing, the cells were filled with those newly charged. Old friends incriminated one another; husbands turned against wives; children against parents. No man trusted his neighbor.

"The Devil is upon us!" a New Yorker wrote to a relative in England. "We lie awake nights listening to the screams of those being dragged off by the constables . . . and wondering when our time will come. . . ."

After a week, Clarke called a stop to the epidemic of charges and countercharges. The confession deadline was moved up to June 26, and those under arrest on that date no longer could purge themselves. "We can't cope with the cases on the docket," a court official lamented. "If this doesn't stop half the city will be behind bars."

Excluded from the voluntary confession amnesty was John Ury. "The papist spy's word will not be accepted were he to name the Pope and all his Cardinals as instigators of the plot. Ury will stand trial and face the judgement of his peers," Governor Clarke said.

With the jail crammed, a sense of calm was restored to the tormented city; although the conspiracy appeared to be frighteningly widespread, relief stemmed from what apparently was the total destruction of the plot and the plotters. Nothing and no one remained under cover. "It has all been brought to the surface!" Bradley exulted.

The prosecutor delayed Ury's trial for several weeks. He questioned Mary Burton many times to clarify the fencing master's role in the scheme; there must be no slip-up in this case. Her responses were confused and vague; in all her previous testimony she had named Hughson as the chief conspirator. In fact, she had not mentioned Ury until Oglethorpe's second letter. Only then had she recalled that the "masked man" visited the tavern on several occasions and given Hughson verbal orders about setting the fires and other matters.

During his pre-trial examination of Mary, Bradley had Ury brought to his office so he could be identified by the star witness. The accused man, wearing a mask, was brought in under heavy guard and commanded to say a few phrases in Latin. But even before he uttered a word, Mary cried, "That's him!"

"Liar! Why are you doing this? You don't even know me!" Ury shouted.

"Yes, yes. That's him. I'd know his voice anywhere," Mary insisted.

"Dear God! Why me?" Ury whispered.

"Remove the mask," Bradley said. The constables obeyed and Ury stood before them, his face reflecting the misery he felt. Mary eyed him without a trace of emotion. There was silence for a long moment, and then Bradley signaled the constables to take Ury away. When the others had left, the prosecutor looked at Mary sharply. "Are you sure that he's the man?" Bradley asked.

"Yes. I'm sure," Mary replied. "Don't worry, Mr. Bradley. He'll swing from a rope. I won't disappoint you in court."

TWELVE

For the first time since the trials had begun, Bradley was seriously concerned because he lacked corroboration of

Mary's testimony. During the period the Attorney General was busy seeking ways to back up her story, a procession of accused men and women passed before Horsmanden for sentencing. In the first three weeks of July, the Judge sent thirteen slaves to the stake and ten more to the gallows, while sixty, including Joanna, Cordelia, and Cato, were shipped to the West Indies. About seventy or eighty were released from custody after making false confessions.

At last Bradley had his campaign against Ury mapped out. He found that William Kane, the soldier, the last of those who had been arrested, was still in jail. Up to that point, Kane had refused to manufacture a confession or to name anyone, insisting that he knew nothing about any plot and had no intentions of playing "squealer." His comrades had not been so high-minded but had seized the chance to get off by branding as conspirators any person who popped into mind.

Apparently Bradley managed to persuade Kane that loss of integrity was preferable to the hangman's rope, for the soldier finally consented to testify in the Ury case as the Attorney General wished. In return for committing perjury, Kane would be released from jail and all charges against him were to be dropped.

The second person Bradley recruited was hapless Sara Hughson. The poor girl was close to a nervous breakdown. Life had turned into a nightmare for her. Led to the gallows three times, she had been reprieved with the noose around her neck.

Bradley came to her cell and offered Sara the choice of

life or death. Either she substantiated Mary Burton's testimony in court or it would be the gallows for her. "I can assure you there will be no reprieve except on my terms. Do as I ask and you'll walk out of here as free as the wind," he said.

Sara was ready to do or say anything; the mere sight of Bradley made her tremble violently. Satisfied that he now had a presentable case, the Attorney General brought Ury to trial on July 22. Hundreds of people packed the courtroom to see and hear the high spot of the conspiracy drama.

Ury provided the initial excitement when he turned down a court-appointed counsel. "I don't trust any lawyer in this city or any man connected with this prejudiced court," he said. "I shall defend myself to the best of my ability."

As events turned out, not even the most brilliant attorney could have saved Ury from the frame-up Bradley had contrived. The prosecutor's methods were neither clever nor subtle, but he had so stacked the cards that he could not lose. The panel from which the jury was chosen held only those men whom Bradley considered to be his supporters. Not even the most persuasive defense lawyer could have swayed them. They already had judged Ury.

Bradley opened his case with a vicious tirade against the Catholic Church, a direct appeal to religious bigotry. Ury's denials that he was a Catholic were met by stony-eyed skepticism. After his opening barrage, the Attorney General called Mary Burton.

With the practiced ease of a seasoned informer, she told the jurors about the "papist ceremonies" Ury had conducted at Hughson's tavern. Her descriptions of them were so farfetched that snickers of laughter came from the audience. It was obvious that Mary's knowledge of Catholicism was purely imaginary. Her overzealousness so embarrassed Bradley that he cut short his direct examination after getting her to testify that Ury, not Hughson, had masterminded the conspiracy.

Until then Mary always had referred to Hughson as the organizer of the plot. She now was contradicting herself. A good lawyer would have demolished her testimony in cross-examination, showed her to be a perjuror and thus blasted Bradley's case. However, Ury was no attorney. He did not even touch upon the inconsistency of the girl's current testimony. Instead he asked her a few trifling questions, which was rather surprising, since Ury was an intelligent and well-educated man—far more intelligent than any of the previous defendants. Possibly he did not know of Mary's previous statements about Hughson and was unaware that any discrepancies existed. His failure to hammer away at the vulnerable witness lost him any slight chance he might have had to save himself.

William Kane followed Mary to the stand with a fantastic story of having been admitted to the conspiracy by Ury and Hughson in a "papist" ritual during which the defendant bound the conspirators to "kill and burn." They needed fear no retribution, Ury had told them, for he claimed to possess the power to forgive sin.

The defendant did not even stoop to challenge this hodgepodge. He seemed stunned by Kane's shameless lies. Sara Hughson then went on the stand, where she gasped affirmative answers to all Bradley's questions, backing Mary Burton and Kane on everything they had stated. She was nearly hysterical and barely coherent. The girl was so shaken that Ury doubted anyone could seriously accept a statement she made. He chivalrously refused to "further torment this poor creature with any queries." Sobbing and wailing, Sara was half carried from the courtroom. That same day she was released from prison, and, a few hours later, leaped into the East River and drowned herself.

In a dramatic and flamboyant style Bradley rested his case by reading to the jury Oglethorpe's letters. The defense was conducted in a dignified and logical manner. Possibly, under normal conditions, Ury would have been acquitted. He presented several respectable character witnesses who swore that his life was blameless, that he was no Catholic and certainly no disguised priest. Other witnesses accounted for Ury's whereabouts at the time he was supposed to have been conducting the rituals at the White Rose Tavern.

The height of Ury's defense was his moving and eloquent summation, delivered with restraint and sincerity. He said in conclusion:

"In the presence of God . . . I lift up my hands and solemnly protest that I am innocent. I never knew or even saw Hughson, his wife, his daughter or the

113

woman hanged with them. . . . I never had any knowledge of a plot or conspiracy. . . . I protest that the witnesses perjured . . . for what reasons and what purposes I leave to their consciences. . . . My own is clear. Gentlemen of the jury! I am innocent!"

His oratory was futile. The jurors took only ten minutes to find him guilty on all counts. He was hanged within a week, and the great conspiracy plot seemed over. But the death of Ury did not end the affair. About fifty slaves were still in jail awaiting trial, and the masters whose bondsmen were imprisoned began clamoring for their release. The authorities could not ignore the growing protests of so many influential men, although Judge Horsmanden, who himself had suffered the loss of three valuable slaves, said of them, ". . . when it comes home to their own houses, the masters close ranks against the investigation . . . yet they were avid to pursue it when others were adversely affected. . . ."

But the Judge's bitterness did not keep Governor Clarke from issuing a general amnesty to all yet held on conspiracy charges. Now that the hysteria had abated, people were starting to wonder how much of it was based on truth. The ugly business had been launched by Mary Burton; was it possible that she had hoodwinked an entire city?

While people were having doubts, Mary again tried to stir up the embers. She attended a session of the grand jury and loosed a series of accusations against certain prominent

New Yorkers, claiming that they were the real leaders, the real brains behind the conspiracy—not Ury or Hughson.

Her charges were so reckless that Attorney General Bradley was "shocked" by her revelations, and Judge Horsmanden, whose trust in her was boundless, admitted that the allegations "staggered one's belief." He ordered the grand-jury minutes suppressed and warned its members never to reveal what they had heard. Exactly what Mary said or whom she accused remained a mystery, but her actions must have convinced the officials that she was unbalanced and could be of no further use to them.

The authorities did not want the facts to be exposed. There would have been tremendous public reaction against the men who had permitted such cruel miscarriages of justice. The investigation of the so-called conspiracy was officially declared at an end.

Mary Burton was paid her reward—not the promised two hundred pounds but five hundred—on the condition that she never more set foot in New York. Mary took her money and disappeared into the shadows of history. Late in August the Provincial Council set aside a day of thanksgiving for "our deliverance from the late conspiracy and its intended massacre. . . ."

After more than two centuries, historians still are uncertain about what actually happened during the dark time of 1741. The identities of the arsonists never were discovered, nor, for that matter, the real purpose behind the fires. The "plot" must remain an unsolved mystery. It probably existed only in the minds of those who tried to profit from it and flourished in the atmosphere of suspicion and fear then current in New York.

However, the Burtons, Bradleys, Clarkes, and Horsmandens have reappeared from time to time in various places and under different guises. Through the centuries they have found eager followers, for those who do not learn from history are condemned to relive it.

INDEX

117

118

119